PASTORAL PSYCHOLOGY
AND INNER CONFLICT

Ioannis K. Kornarakis

PASTORAL PSYCHOLOGY AND INNER CONFLICT

Translated by Esther Williams

HOLY CROSS ORTHODOX PRESS
Brookline, Massachusetts

Published by Holy Cross Orthodox Press
50 Goddard Avenue
Brookline, Massachusetts 02146

Cover design by Mary C. Vaporis

Library of Congress Cataloging-in-Publication Data

Kornarakis, Ioannis K.
[Encheiridion Poimantikēs Psychologias. English]
Pastoral psychology and inner conflict/Ioannis K. Kornarakis;
translated by Esther Williams.
p.   cm.
Translation of: Encheiridion Poimantikēs Psychologias.
Includes bibliographical references and index.
ISBN 0-917651-78-2
1. Pastoral psychology. 2. Orthodox Eastern Church — Doctrines.
3. Psychoanalysis and religion. 4. Spiritual direction. I. Title.
BV4012.K6613   1990   90-43815
253.5'2—dc20   CIP

CONTENTS

FOREWORD

Pastoral psychology, a specialized scientific branch of academic theology, has two basic characteristics: a) It is a new scientific pastoral discipline. b) Since it is organically dependent upon the constantly developing science of psychology, its subject matter cannot, at least as yet, be firmly outlined.

These characteristics make it difficult or impossible to define precisely the content and scope of the course to be offered to students. As we know, psychological research is concerned with the whole field of the various actions and reactions of the human personality. The psychological problems of human behavior are boundless.

Part One outlines the main psychological, existential problems of the human personality from the point of view of Orthodox theology. This will be followed by a second part to deal with pastoral problems arising from the particular psychological appraisals of certain human reactions in interpersonal relations.

INTRODUCTION

PASTORAL PSYCHOLOGY

The broad field of psychological research includes many specialized branches, such as developmental psychology, social phychology, the psychology of religion, and so forth. One such discipline, pastoral psychology, is concerned with applying the findings of contemporary psychological theories to the pastoral work of the Church. It makes use of general psychological knowledge within the spiritual work of the Church.

Pastoral psychology then may be defined as the methodical study of psychic processes or facts in the light of the needs and demands of the pastoral work of the Church. In its theory and practice pastoral psychology is certainly not unknown in the history of theology and the life of the Church. In our time, however, because of the new scientific awareness of particular areas of the psychological life of the human personality, pastoral psychology is becoming established as a specialized psychological discipline which aims to improve the pastoral work of the Church with respect to its anthropological assumptions and possibilities. Pastoral psychology is a part of the human effort required for the fulfilment of the conditions for salvation as defined in Orthodox teaching. In this sense the purpose in establishing pastoral psychology as a branch of Orthodox academic theology is to inquire into the potentialities of the latter in the specific area of pastoral studies.

The Relationship Between Academic Theology and Pastoral Psychology.

Of course it is not a new discovery that academic theology is related to psychology. In a special study made by Professor Nicholas

Louvaris entitled *The Psychology of Religion and its Relation to Theology* one can follow the development of this relationship and see its potential where religious psychological material is being interpreted.

The problem of whether and to what degree psychological research has to do with man's religious experience began to appear at the time of the first attempts to apply psychological knowledge to the study of religious experience. Then discussions began whether psychology could be applied in this way and what the practical or theoretical consequences would be for theology and the life of the Church. One result of these discussions was the creation of a chair of the psychology of religion at the Theological School of the University of Athens. This, however, was abolished not long afterwards and was amalgamated with the chair of the philosophy of religion.

This prehistory of the relation between psychology and academic theology makes still clearer the special scientific character of pastoral psychology in relation to academic theology. As we have pointed out elsewhere, the fact that the psychology of religion preceded pastoral psychology, and especially the fact that 'the psychology of religion contributes only to defining psychologically the peculiarities of the religious phenomenon' (Troeltsch),[2] bring out the essential difference in the work of these two psychologies and hence in their relations to academic theology. According to Louvaris, 'Psychology (of religion) is able to demonstrate the texture of religious awareness and hence the essence of religion as well as its independence of the values of the true, the beautiful and the good, in contrast to the other fields of the spiritual life. Thus it also becomes clear that religion has its own foundation, as do the arts and ethics.'[3] These achievements of the psychology of religion relate it directly to the systematic branch of academic theology.

It is clear, on the other hand, that pastoral psychology is directly connected with the practical branch of academic theology. For, as we have indicated in the above definition, pastoral psychology is not concerned with theoretical problems such as the texture of religious awareness, the essence of religion or its independence, but with psychological problems which have a direct bearing on the individual's effort to live by the truth of the Gospel in his practical life. Therefore, while the psychology of religion belongs to the systematic branch of academic theology, pastoral psychology belongs to its practical branch.

The Relation of Psychology to the Spiritual Life

The advance of psychology, and the study of man's existential problems in the light of its findings, confront pastoral psychology with the question: How does the Orthodox tradition understand and define the relationship of psychology to the spiritual life?

Before this question can be answered, three matters must be clarified: a) What is a 'psychological fact' (psychology)? b) What is a 'spiritual fact' (the spiritual life)? c) How far is it possible to fix a boundary between these two areas of human existence?

a) What is a psychological fact? — A psychological fact is a subjective human experience which is described, analyzed and interpreted purely in terms of the functioning of the psyche in itself, that is to say without reference to values. The term 'psychological fact' refers to the functioning and actions of the dynamic elements of the psyche, either in self-contained expression or interrelated and interdependent.

Every person has his 'psychological side.' He has his purely subjective experience which define his individual identity on the 'psychological side.' His psychic world functions within the framework and capacities of his personal 'psychological' identity. He has his feelings, his desires, his emotional frustrations, disappointments, joys and sorrows. Thus a desire, an instinctive impulse, a volitional act or a functioning of the intellect as belonging to the capacities of the human psyche, are psychological facts. All of these psychic effects, in a correlation and interdependence that are peculiar each time, are psychic dynamisms which are expressed in concrete biomatic[4] forms of human action and reaction. For instance, the way in which two individuals relate to each other — such as the feelings of a father, mother, son or daughter, those of a subordinate towards his employer, the imposition of paternal authority — are examples of psychic dynamisms which are understood in the first instance as psychological facts.

These phychological facts constitute the structural elements of the individual's human problem. But this human problem does not consist only of psychological facts. It is also an expression of the dynamic spiritual configuration of his personality.

b) What is a spiritual fact? — The term 'spiritual fact' or 'spiritual life' is capable of many interpretations, depending on the content of the concept 'spirit.'

In the context of pastoral psychology the term 'spiritual fact' has reference to the charismatic operation of the Holy Spirit. In this sense it is a spiritual fact to live by the workings of the Holy Spirit; a Christian's sharing in the life of the Holy Spirit is a spiritual fact.

c) What kind of boundary can be drawn between psychological and spiritual facts? — The distinction is not easy to make, but we can explore its possibilities in the framework of the Apostle Paul's teaching about the natural-carnal man and the spiritual man. According to this teaching, without the Holy Spirit a man remains carnal, that is 'natural.' His psychic functions and his subjective experience are *natural* psychological events, unrelated to the life of the Holy Spirit.

Yet it is also true that while a psychological function or a dynamic motion of the psyche, a subjective experience (a weakness, a decision, a thought, etc.) may in the first instance have no real relation to the life in Christ, still it has a definite position, neutral or negative, with respect to that life. Therefore even a denial of the spiritual life, through any psychological expression or action whatever, is a form of spiritual life which enables us (albeit in a negative way) to make a comparison between the person's psychological behaviour and the life in the Holy Spirit.

We must not forget, especially in pastoral psychology, that a sinner under the guidance of a pastor is on his way towards spiritual rebirth and therefore is participating in the life of the Holy Spirit. This means that this person is not only carnal (natural), nor only spiritual. He has in operation his human spiritual dynamisms which the Church tries to sanctify and enlist in a *spiritual* struggle to reshape the image of the sinner into the 'image of God.'

Therefore we must characterize a subjective experience (or a psychological dynamism) as a 'psychological fact' when we see it as a human capacity. At the same time we must recognize it as a 'spiritual fact' when we attach it directly and organically to the life of the Holy Spirit. (Prayer, participation in the sacraments, acts of charity, of consolation, of facing temptation, etc., are spiritual facts with a psychological, human substratum.)

Finally, we can understand that every spiritual fact always has a psychological foundation, a human substructure. In confronting pastoral problems, pastoral psychology tries to single out the underlying psychological substructure beneath the 'spiritual facts' of the human personality. The study of this substructure in isolation can make authentic living by the operations of the Holy Spirit much easier to attain. For if the pastor does not recognize what is a psychological fact or a human capacity (or weakness) when dealing with a pastoral problem, he will be reduced to confusion, possibly error, and pastoral failure. So he must know the boundaries which mark the relationship between psychology and the spiritual life.

It should be noted that in the field of pastoral psychology the term 'psychology' is ideologically neutral. It is not limited to contemporary psychological findings but is concerned with the scientific research of any epoch which studies the psychodynamic elements of the human personality. Taking the term 'psychology' in this broad sense facilitates further the correlation of psychology with the spiritual life as understood in the Orthodox tradition. The psychology which interests us here is not exlusively that of Freud, Jung, Adler or Aristotle. Precisely, it is the general scientific discipline which studies man's subjective experiences as the effects of operations within the psyche, independent of the broader existential connections which involve the element of value or 'world outlook.'

The Relationship between Depth Psychology
and the Work of Spiritual Counseling.

Those psychological theories which have the scientific aim of studying and understanding the depth of the human psyche are together characterized as depth psychology. The psychological theories of Freud, Adler and Jung are regarded as basic theories, or schools, of depth psychology, since their conclusions relate to psychical phenomena which are not directly accessible to the consciousness of the persons in whom they occur.

Psychological research up to the time of Freud was concerned with the study of conscious psychical phenomena and the conscious functions of the psyche. That research could be characterized as surface psychology, since its scientific work was based on the then common notion that man is what he appears to be. Man's psychic reactions were regarded as the simple consequences of stimuli from the environment and therefore as psychical phenomena subject to psychological laws which could be determined with precision. The discrepancies between different scholars' findings were ascribed more to the problem of their methods of inquiry than to the interior state of man. Nor did the ever burning question of the relationship between heredity and environment, or the individual constitution and the environment, raise suspicions of another side of the personality in which the origin of psychical phenomena might be found. Every psychological reaction which could not be interpreted on the basis of stimuli coming from the environment was attributed to heredity and to the individual constitution. Thus psychological research had the point of view of a surface psychology.

By contrast, the scientific aims of depth psychology are firmly oriented towards that psychical region of the human personality which is not directly conscious in the individual. This area of the psyche is regarded as the *depth* of the human personality, and it is here that the psychological processes which determine and motivate human behaviour take place and develop. Therefore depth psychology acknowledges that man is not what he seems. According to this psychology, the real person is hidden within psychological processes which are inaccessible to direct scientific experience and take place in the depth of the human personality. So the purpose of depth psychology is to discover ways of approaching the depths of the human personality and to study and interpret the deep psychodynamic elements which determine and dictate human behavior.

The purpose of depth psychology explains well enough why efforts are being made to use its findings in the work of spiritual guidance. For if, as we have said, the Christian (or any person) is first of all a psychodynamic entity, a being with psychodynamic

motives, actions and reactions, it is an advantage for the pastor
to be as familiar as possible with the nature and special characteristics of these dynamic elements of the psyche. Indeed the
most fundamental problem in the work of spiritual counseling is
really the question of how *genuine*[5] the person's spiritual life is.
If the pastor confines his guidance to the surface of a person's
psychic life, he will be unable to discern the authenticity of the
'seeming' manifestations of spiritual life in him. In many cases
what is characterized as spiritual life may really be nothing but
an unconscious form of psychic disharmony, weakness or illness.
P. Daco's observation that 'illnesses have become spiritual ways
of life'[6] is no mistake or exaggeration. A complex or hidden aggression may be expressed in the psychological 'dress' of a
virtue[7] and thus lead the pastor to an erroneous judgement and
so to inappropriate pastoral behavior or guidance.

Of course pastoral counselling develops within the charismatic
activity of the life of the Church, and no one maintains that
psychological knowledge is the sole means by which the pastor can
approach the immense depth of the human personality. But if, as
we have suggested elsewhere, the pastor is not a spiritual father
endowed with perfect discernment, he is nevertheless obliged, as
an instrument of God's grace, to use his human capacities to work
in creative cooperation with God's grace. Psychological knowledge
is an indirect gift of God to his aspiring, conscientious and faithful
co-worker.

Even supposing that a pastor was very 'clear-sighted' and 'perfect in things spiritual' (like Abba Moses, for example), we could
not understand his method of spiritual guidance without going
deeply into the personality of the individual receiving his guidance
and pastoral care. Here too it is useful to make a distinction (a
historical one, for the present) between contemporary depth psychology and pastoral depth psychology. The latter, as we shall see further on, constitutes experience lived within the pastoral work of the
Orthodox Church. The current scientific awareness of depth psychology naturally calls to mind the history of similar efforts made by
pastors who believed, with Saint Makarios of Egypt, that 'the soul
has many parts and much depth.'[8] By inquiring deeply into the
human personality, contemporary depth psychology contributes

to man's effort to know himself — for most people do not know themselves and therefore are not sincere either with themselves or with others. Pastoral depth psychology in the Orthodox tradition also takes this path of revealing the illusion which the spiritual person may be mistaking for authentic truth in his way of life. Saint Makarios of Egypt makes a similar point: 'See how you deceive yourself, because you imagine that you believe, when you do not yet believe as you ought in truth.'[9]

It is clear, then, that the work of spiritual guidance which was practised in the past by the Fathers of the Church, and is also practised today by discriminating and conscientious pastors, is directly concerned with the depth of the psyche. Therefore the Church is encouraged to use the findings of contemporary scientific depth psychology in her work of spiritual guidance. In this sense pastoral psychology is to be understood mainly as pastoral depth psychology.

The Confessional Character of Pastoral Psychology

Pastoral psychology as a particular branch of academic theology appeared first in Protestant Christianity. That was a natural result not only of the advances in psychology but also of the nature of the pastoral work in the Protestant communities generally.

As we work, that work is still developing within the framework of Protestant doctrinal teaching. While it is true that in Protestant communities the acts of charity and love towards their members are always rich in extent and quality of expression, yet those things in themselves are insufficient to meet the deeper psychological and spiritual needs of their members. It must be emphasized that the absence of the sacrament of Confession and of the counselling which is organically connected with it is a fundamental deficiency in the Protestant pastoral field. The Protestant pastor cannot avail himself of the rich soteriological possibilities of the sacrament of Confession if this sacrament is rejected in the doctrinal teaching of his community. His effort is then limited to a 'counselling' activity. His good influence on the members of his parish depends basically on the use of 'human relations,' 'emotional contact,' 'understanding of the neighbor' and the personal encounter in general. This is why pastors of Protestant communities have turned with such interest to the new developments in psychology and the anthropological sciences in general. Psychology has given them a better chance of success in entering into another person's feelings. The psychological dialogue in particular, as a therapeutic and 'redemptive' method, has encouraged many Protestant pastors to proceed to acquire the capacity for empathy, supported by the achievements of psychoanalysis.

Interestingly enough, the historian of pastoral psychology rightly points out that this psychology began in Europe in the period during which the works of the Protestant pastor Oskar Pfister appeared, whose book *Christianity and Anxiety*[10] (remarkable for the time) accepted Freudian psychoanalysis absolutely and identified it unconditionally with his pastoral work. This fact alone shows that a pastoral psychology cannot be understood apart from its confessional presuppositions and conditions.

The 'confessional problem' of pastoral psychology can be comprehended more easily if three things are taken into account: a) the large *number* of psychological theories and views about the basic characteristics or functions of the human psyche (and therefore the *disagreements* among the proponents of these theories), b) the overstepping of the psychological theories by scientists who extend them unjustifiably into the realm of man's 'world outlook' and metaphysical quests, and c) the special character of pastoral service as a soteriological activity which grows within the framework of the 'unveiling in Christ.'

These three basic structural elements of the confessional problem of pastoral psychology point to three fundamental problems which must be succesfully dealt with before modern psychological ideas and findings can be used in pastoral work with success, that is without distorting its confessional character: a) the *selection* of useful psychological ideas and findings, b) the *extent* of the data which can be used pastorally, and c) the *way* in which psychological knowledge is to be applied to concrete pastoral problems. If these questions can be worked out successfully in each pastoral situation, then the Orthodox confessional character of the pastoral psychology applied in this situation can be assured, and it can therefore be characterized as Orthodox pastoral psychology.

The confessional problem of pastoral psychology, examined in the light of its historical beginning as a self-conscious discipline, proves to be extraordinarily complex. But as we have already said, the problem can also be confronted by tracing the traditional pastoral psychological work done by the Church in the past. The use of 'modern' psychological achievements by pastoral psychology makes particularly emphatic the confessional problem involved. But the fact that psychological knowledge has previously been used to a certain extent in the pastoral activity of the Church makes this problem less acute. For if the modern achievements in the field of scientific depth psychology (Freud, Adler, Jung and others) are not the only source of pastoral psychological material, but simply one source among others, the confessional problem of pastoral psychology can easily be solved on the basis of the terms which define the nature and function of an Orthodox pastoral psychology.

ORTHODOX PASTORAL PSYCHOLOGY

The only source of pastoral psychology developed and applied within the Protestant community is psychological science, with related anthropological disciplines such as medicine, psychiatry and psychotherapy, which offer the possibility of making use of psychological problems in connection with the basic human problem. Pastoral psychology in the West generally lacks the wealth of anthropological and psychological tradition which modern Orthodox pastoral psychology is able to call upon. If the latter is only now becoming aware of itself as a particular scientific branch of pastoral theology, yet it has its prehistory going back to the spiritual experience of the Fathers of the Church, the lives of saints, the rich tradition of worship and generally the anthropological presuppositions and conditions of the spiritual life of the Orthodox East. The following are sources of Orthodox pastoral psychology:

1. *Holy Scripture* (*The Old and New Testaments*).
Holy Scripture, the book of man *par excellence*, contains biomatic patterns of human behavior which are characterized by their existential immediacy. That is, they are not 'contrived' or 'fabricated'[11] in order to achieve a specific purpose, as may happen in psychological writings aimed at supporting the writer's

particular psychological thesis. The psychological 'finds' in the pages of the Bible are always natural and spontaneous reactions of the human psyche within the setting in which it is functioning. Moreover, since the history and reality of the human personality in his relations with God and the world is contained in the pages of Holy Scripture, the psychological structures of human behavior found in those pages bear the seal of biblical authority. These structures can be characterized as 'archetypal,' because they usually present basic types of behavior and are expressed with precision. For instance, one can speak of the 'Adam complex,' the 'scapegoat complex,' the 'Esau complex' and others. These 'archetypal' psychological structures of the human personality are keys which can open up the barriers to understanding the personality when one is dealing with basic pastoral problems.

Here too we must remember that attention needs to be given to the method of clarifying a psychological structure which is 'concealed' within the pages of the Bible. The methodology of discovering and clarifying such a structure should be dictated by conditions which will safeguard the unique integrity of the biblical experience or event in which these structures are contained. In any case it is certain that whatever advances are made in psychology and other anthropological studies in the present or future, their findings will always be useful for a deeper and broader clarification of the psychological structures of the human behavior contained in the Bible. This fact indicates the inestimable value of the biblical text as a source of Orthodox pastoral psychology.

2. The Works of the Fathers and Writers of the Church

It is self-evident that the Fathers of the Church are still the authentic and expert pastors of the Christian congregation. Those of them who have at any time put their pastoral experience into writing or whose biographies have been written by other Fathers and writers of the Church constitute, by their personal lives, their service and their writings, an important source of pastoral psychological material.

Here we should also point out that the emphasis on the significance of the Fathers' psychological knowledge is not part of a church education which is alien and unrelated to education generally as it is conceived and understood in the contemporary world of psychology and education. When the well known foreign patristic scholar Irenaeus Hausherr points to Maximos the Confessor as 'the forerunner of depth psychology thirteen centuries ago'[12] it is easy to understand that the 'psychological knowledge' of the Church Fathers is precisely human knowledge gained not only in the field of practical life but also in theoretical inquiries. This fact adds special weight to the limpid psychological analysis and synthesis which one finds in the patristic texts.

The ascetic writings more particularly, however, are important for pastoral psychology. Most of the ascetic writings contain descriptions and analyses of introspective states occurring in the arena of intensive asceticism and prayer. In these descriptions and analyses it is often possible to follow the actions and reactions of the hidden psychic faculties and functions and therefore to understand more easily the nature and scope of the relations between spiritual counselling and developments in modern psychology. If a deep and extensive methodical study of the ascetic writings by the psychological investigator reveal that the psychological knowledge gained from these texts is no less timely and significant than modern achievements in psychology, he will understand that the psychological wealth of the patristic writings and the prevailing psychological findings of our time form a unified field from which to draw pastoral psychological material.

3. *The Lives of Saints of the Church.*
The 'conduct' of the faithful contenders who are finally crowned with the crown of holiness is always rich in reactions transparent to the inner spiritual and psychical states of man's personality. Psychology, and especially the psychology of religion, has been interested in studying the lives of the prominent saints who were great men and women of action. Special interest is certainly being shown in the saints' mystical experiences, which are the innermost (and therefore essentially unsearchable) spiritual states in the religious life.

4. *The Church's Life of Worship as Reflected in its Liturgical Books.*
The liturgical books of the Church are also a source of pastoral

psychological material, reflecting the anthropological and charismatic dimensions of the life of worship.

As we know, worship is the center and source of the spiritual life of the Church. The great number of services and sacramental ceremonies has been enriched with a vast amount of hymnographic and liturgical material in general. The hymnography and prayers in the liturgical texts express the human element, and describe and analyze it. With an inspiration sanctified by asceticism and prayer, hymnographers and melodists have managed, in an inexhaustible variety of expressions, to present the inner elements of the personality of the religious individual.

Here we should perhaps emphasize particularly the prominence of the inner biomatic states of the psyche in the pages of the *Triodion*. The man of the *Triodion* is not simply a man of prayer. He is a man who suffers, who prays struggling and struggles praying. His life is a life of vigilance and sobriety. His most basic problem is sin, a continual life of sin. But there is repentance too, a continual life of repentance. He lives in sin and repentance at the same time. He is aware of his wretchedness but also of his greatness. He feels his abandonment to the powers of corruption and sin, but also feels how he is lifted up by the mercy and love of God.

The study of the man of the *Triodion* is exceedingly useful and fundamental for understanding the existential border states in the life of the religious man. The psychological (and spiritual) anatomy of the individual struggling against the corruption due to sin is always a rich source of pastoral psychological material, which is, moreover, sealed with the authority of tradition. For much as the existential problems of contemporary man differ from those of men of the past, the structure of these problems will always remain the same, since this structure has resulted irrevocably from man's fall into the vicious circle of a sinful way of life. Therefore what has crystalized hymnographically and liturgically in the long tradition of worship in the life of the Church is always an exceptionally important source for pastoral psychological material. But it is mainly in the hymnographic wealth of the *Triodion* that the most sensitive and therefore deepest recesses of the pastoral religious life are discovered. Against modern man's despair and bitterness over his 'tragic' 'impasse,' the Orthodox pastor can marshal the experience of the bitterness of sin suffered by the sinner and yet also his certainty of a redemptive way out of the 'impasse' in which sin has encaged him. In the two cases the subjective experiences as 'psychological facts' are related and 'similar.' They have the same psychological (existential) depth and pathos. They differ only in existential outlook.

These two sets of existential experiences, that of the man driven to despair by his 'tragic' 'impasse' and that of the religious man of the *Triodion*, likewise create a unified source for pastoral psychological material.

A more general survey will readily show that the area in which the subjective experience of the religious man opens out most widely is the area of worship. Therefore what has crystallized in the liturgical texts expresses in an authoritative (traditional) way the depth and breadth of these experiences. Hence these texts constitute an important source of pastoral psychological material.

5. *Practical Pastoral Experience*

The experience which the pastor acquires in the course of his work is a fundamental source of pastoral psychology. This experience can be differentiated with respect to its origin into two superimposed layers of sources of pastoral psychological material.

a) *The scientific experience of the pastor.* Since pastoral psychology constitutes a special *scientific* discipline within the broader science of psychology, the 'spiritual director' is obliged to make a *methodical* investigation of pastoral problems, provided that he possesses sound psychological knowledge. Certainly this work is not for every pastor, but as we have emphasized, it is for the spiritual director who would like to bring his work up to date from the point of view of utilizing the psychological advances of his time.

b) *The pastoral experience of the pastor.* The most authentic source of pastoral psychological material is undoubtedly the pastor's direct pastoral experience. This material may later be elaborated methodically in order to define pastoral psychological laws. The pastor who has a conscious pastoral psychological perspective can collect material consisting of instances illustrating characteristic pastoral psychological problems which will be studied scientifically *a posteriori* by a competent investigator.

This method of acquiring pastoral psychological material is a direct recognition of the essential role of pastoral psychology. For it is from this practice that the need arises for a pastoral psychological perspective of methodology in pastoral work. That is to say that if the pastor's practical experience spontaneously creates his need for special psychological preparation in order to meet his pastoral problems more effectively, it is easier to recognize the value of practising pastoral psychology in a methodical way.

A further reason for emphasizing the prime importance of practical pastoral experience for collecting pastoral psychological material is that this experience, when lived fully, is at the same time a participation in the charismatic texture of pastoral work. As long as the pastoral psychological perspective isolates the 'psychological facts' in order to explain man's possibilities for doing the work of spiritual edification, it is not necessary facing (as pastoral experience) the whole breadth and depth of pastoral practice, which is a result of cooperation between the divine and human factors. But the practical experience of the pastor, lived within the whole framework of this cooperation, can get to know the importance of the human side (the human possibilities as 'psychological facts') for achieving positive and fruitful collaboration between the divine and human factors. More simply, in the practice of his apostolate the pastor can more easily comprehend the benefit of understanding the believer's subjective experiences as 'psychological facts.' At the same time, through his practical experience he can understand better the divine claim on man's cooperation (as far as possible) in the work of spiritual edification and salvation. The 'discerning' fathers are preeminently those who count on the psychodynamic 'mechanisms' of the human personality to play a positive role in the work of the salvation of soul.

6. *Psychology and its Application in the Specialized Therapeutic Branches, i.e. Psychotherapy and Psychiatry.*

According to what has been said so far, psychology, including its application in psychotherapy, counselling, psychiatry and all the other areas of guidance, is the fundamental source of pastoral psychological material.

In general, psychological research and the practical application of its findings are of direct interest to the pastoral psychological
investigator. Since general psychology and pastoral psychology have
one and the same object, man, the findings of psychology and their
applications to different areas of man's problem are obvious sources
of pastoral psychological material. In spite of the fact that their
scientific orientations, their goals, and above all, their perspectives on the human problems which they face are different, the
material which psychology collects in the course of its research
is particularly important for pastoral psychology.

At this point we must emphasize the special value of the
psychological material gathered in the first phase of a scientific
psychological investigation. The aim of the investigation is of course
to collect the material and afterwards to study it on the basis of
the patricular scientific presuppositions and pursuits of the
psychological school concerned. The material derived from
methodical (scientific) psychological research is a reality given by
the nature of the functioning of the human personality. Before
this material has been analyzed and investigated on the basis of
the scientific presuppositions and aims of the particular psychological school, it can be used in a similar way by pastoral
psychological research. For instance, the psychological events (examples) interpreted by a particular psychological school of thought
are usually the products of 'objective' observations, of an unbiased
(up to a point) scientific orientation. That is, if a psychological
description, or even an analysis, gives us the picture of a jealous
spouse, this description and analysis are of direct interest to the
pastoral psychological investigator, because they form a picture
of a definite piece of psychological behavior. This picture can be
used in a pastoral psychological way.

A special problem is created for the pastoral psychologist when
a piece of psychological behavior such as this picture of the jealous
spouse is *interpreted* in terms of a particular psychological school
of thought. For instance, the picture in question can be interpreted
psychologically on the basis of the Oedipus complex or it can be
interpreted according to Jung's principles, especially his theory
of the *anima* and the *animus*. At this point the particular presuppositions of pastoral psychological science will determine which

interpretion will harmonize better with the psychospiritual character of the human personality and the aims of pastoral work. The pastoral psychologist can accept one or the other interpretation or reject both of them.

This position taken by the pastoral psychologist certainly cannot be characterized as unscientific on the argument that he has no right to show 'disrespect' for the theoretical principles and conclusions of one psychological school — that is, to accept one of its principles and reject another. The nature of psychological research is such that almost no psychological theory can be applied even by its first followers exactly as taught by its author. Since, as Jung himself emphasized, the basic problem of psychological research is that its subject (the investigator) and its object (what is investigated) are one and the same, that is man, the psychological interpretations of the same psychic event is naturally also a function of the subjective states of its plurality of investigators. This interpretive difficulty alone readily explains why followers of one school split off in particular scientific directions clearly different from those of the founder. To apply a psychological theory with absolute theoretical consistency over a long period of years would in fact be to condemn its scientific work to a standardization which would clearly be both unscientific and unpsychological.

For the above reasons the pastoral psychologist too has scientific freedom to make a selection on the basis of the particular theoretical presuppositions of his work, not only from the psychological materials gathered by 'outside' psychological research, but also from the interpretations arrived at by the different schools of thought.

7. Methodical Pastoral Psychological Research

Another source for gathering pastoral psychological material is, of course, the methodical scientific psychological research done by the pastoral psychologist within the framework of practical pastoral psychological problems. The gathering of this material is especially important, as in the case of the methodical efforts of the 'spiritual director,' because it concerns contemporary pastoral psychological experiences. As we have said, the pastoral psychological material drawn from written sources of the past is fundamentally important for the Orthodox research worker. But it is easy to understand the *timeliness* of the pastoral psychological material which a specialist collects from the fields of the psychological knowledge of his time. Despite the fact that man's basic existential problems are always the same, since they have been irrevocably determined by man's fall into sin (the nature of sin is always the same and unchanging from the time when it 'entered the world'), the particular aspects of these problems always depend on the concrete psychological conditions of the epoch in which they are experienced. Holy Scripture, too, naturally lays stress on the instability of human life, the inevitability of the changes to which this life is subject and the variability of men's psychic dispositions as a result of the external conditions in which they live. Therefore the problems connected with living according to the Gospel and its truth change all the time, not because of any change in the theoretical truths of the faith, which are always the same, but because of the new psychosocial conditions and the general spirit of each epoch. This fact compels pastoral psychological research to gather contemporary psychological material which will throw more light on the nature of the present-day problems of living according to the Gospel.

At this point we should emphasize the special role which the subjective experiences of the pastoral psychologist can play in methodical psychological research. Since this research is bound up with the problem of the identity of the subject (the investigator) with the object (what he investigates), the religious psychodynamic content of the pastoral psychologist's personality inevitably becomes a source of pastoral psychological material. The psychodynamic factors of his personality inevitably produce ideas, interpretations, definitions and other psychological elements with their own significance as pastoral psychological material.

Criteria of the Theory and Practice of Orthodox Pastoral Psychology.

In order to be in confessional harmony with Orthodox Christian teaching and with the life and saving action of the Orthodox Church in general, the theory and practice of pastoral psychology must be based on Orthodox dogmatic (anthropological and soterio-logical) principles. The following are the main criteria which together can define the possibilities and the framework of the theory and practice of Orthodox pastoral psychology:

1. *Orthodox dogma.* The dogmatic teaching of the Orthodox Church is the primary, essential basis of Orthodox pastoral psychology. While the latter is a special psychological discipline with regard to its scientific function and perspective, the purpose of its theory and practice is organically united with Orthodox dogma. Orthodox pastoral psychology has the aim of serving the pastoral purposes which are defined by this dogma. Therefore, for instance, it is impossible for this psychology to embrace in its theory of the structure of the human psyche the theoretical principles of Jung's psychology which offer an 'enrichment' of the trinitarian Christian dogma by a further principle (the devil or the Virgin Mary) in order that the triad should be completed in a tetrad or in order to give us a 'union of opposites' (*compositio oppositorum).* The adulteration of Orthodox Christian dogma in the area of the psychology of the human personality would mean the adulteration of the aims of the Christian life which this dogma defines. In any case such an adulteration would lead to a substantial and radical misdirection of pastoral psychology and would render it incapable of carrying out the aims imposed by the nature of its pastoral identity.[14]

2. *Orthodox anthropology.* The Orthodox Church has a definite teaching and theory concerning man, albeit in very general outlines. Its anthropology is safeguarded dogmatically and has a normal place in the framework of pastoral activity. A vigorous develop-ment (clarification) of its anthropological theories always assumes the presence of these dogmatic boundaries as its framework. For this reason, in spite of the fact that our time is characterized by a lively interest in anthropology and therefore by a constant ac-cumulation of anthropological findings, Orthodox dogmatic teaching can find only a few of these conclusions conformable to its anthropological principles. The pastoral psychologist must be motivated by the dogmatic anthropological basis of Orthodox Chris-tian teaching as he tries to select the positive anthropological knowledge of our time.

3. *Orthodox morals.* We know that the rigorous scientific stand on the principles which must govern psychological research strictly rule out any organic correlating of psychological phenomena with human morals[15] which are expressed in the person's values. Yet the very people who have introduced basic psychological theories make reference (sometimes positive, sometimes negative) to the role which an individual's moral awareness plays in the origin and development of psychological phenomena or in the human psyche as a whole. For instance, Erich Fromm,[16] as a champion of humanistic psychological ethics, maintains that he is creating 'a new ethics' and consequently new human morals. In cases like Fromm's, in which psychology offers 'new morals,' it oversteps its jurisdiction and, without seeming to realize it, slips into realm of a philosophy of life. For this reason Orthodox pastoral psychology bases itself directly upon Orthodox morals. For this psychology is a 'psychology of morals' by its very nature, in that it aims to serve pastoral purposes.

4. *Orthodox soteriology.* The general notion of pastoral care of the faithful of course includes all the pedagogic, healing-corrective and soteriological activities of the Church. Orthodox pastoral psychology aims especially to serve these purposes as a part of the general redemptive action of the Church. The contribution of this psychology to the work of making the individual aware of his mental states and clarifying them can be used pedagogically, therapeutically and finally *soteriologically.* Therefore Orthodox pastoral psychology cannot accept indiscriminately the psychological conclusions which are directly connected with the 'therapeutic' aims of 'scientific psychology.' Nor can it propose the adoption of psychotherapeutic methods which depend directly and exclusively on those conclusions. Orthodox soteriology will always remain the firm basis for deciding what 'therapeutic' use to make of the conclusions of contemporary psychology.

The main thing to bear in mind here is the essential and unbridgeable gap which separates the 'therapeutic' aims of psychotherapeutic education from the redemptive aims of pastoral work. Psychotherapeutic 'soteriology' is relative and indeed in many cases questionable. Its exclusive dependence on unconscious and imponderable inner processes often involves it in problems requiring long-term treatment which ultimately remains ineffectual.

For its part, pastoral psychology clearly has faith in the pastoral value of psychological knowledge, but this faith is clearly subordinated to the charismatic possibilities of pastoral work. As we have said, psychological knowledge and its use represent one part of man's collaboration in the work of his salvation. But as this collaboration develops, the 'other factor' has the initiative and the limitless possibilities of a soteriological process which may go above and beyond the significance and value of that knowledge. Let us not forget that 'with God nothing will be impossible' (Lk 1.37)!

THE PASTORAL PSYCHOLOGIST

It is clear from what has been said so far that the person of the pastoral psychologist, especially the dynamic religious content of his personality, is a conditioning factor in the making of an Orthodox pastoral psychology.

Indeed almost every piece of work that is done is organically and directly connected with the mentality of the person who does it. The special aspects of the work done, its quality, quantity and extent, as well as its results in terms of the goal pursued, depend directly upon the subjective experiences and personal motivations of the worker. The relationship of the worker to his work is a psychological dialectic which causes the worker to influence or shape the work in correlation with his general subjective dispositions and states, and the work correspondingly influences the subjectivity of the worker. This psychological dialectical relationship is witnessed clearly and more directly in the relationship of the pastoral psychologist to the object of his investigation.

This realization already determines the basis for a scientific method of pastoral psychological research. All of the prerequisites for the psychological research worker are indispensable for the person doing research in Orthodox pastoral psychology. Properly the pastoral psychologist must have the formal scientific preparation of a conscientious and capable student of psychology. But beyond these 'scientific' prerequisites, the pastoral psychologist must have qualifications peculiar to the pastoral nature of his work. Furthermore, he must constantly enrich his subjective religious experiences with the experience of living by the truths of the Gospel in the midst of the struggle and activity of everyday life. If pastoral psychology really is the field of theoretical confrontation, by study and interpretation of the practical (existential psychological) problems of the religious man, he who works theoretically must inevitably draw his theory (either to confirm of deny it) also from whatever participation he has in the experience of these problems. Of course the pastoral psychologist cannot have direct experience of all the problems of the religious person, and this breadth of experience is not what we mean when we speak of the significance of his subjective religious experience for the progress of his work. Nevertheless, no pastoral psychologist is fit for this type of work if he has no part in the way of life of the gospel truths or remains a cold student of these truths. Any existential dissociation from this way of life will limit his 'scientific' pastoral psychological knowledge. But then his work will lie outside the field of Orthodox pastoral problems.

The pastoral psychological investigator must possess and increase the experience of living his gospel truths in organic connection with the traditional Orthodox view of life. This condition does not in the first instance aim at a restraining conservatism. It only emphasizes the universality of the existential outlook of the religious person. For what has heretofore been lived by the congregation of the Church, and especially by its saints, is not only a source of pastoral psychological material, as we have said, but also a biomatic, existential continuity which defines the nature and character of the authentic religious experiences of every period. The psychosocial conditions of each epoch may change, or the pastoral activity of the Church may become different in its methodological perspectives, but the Orthodox view of life always remains the biomatic basis of its activity.

PART ONE

CHAPTER ONE

THE ORIGINS OF THE PSYCHIC CONFLICT

In recent decades it has been the main purpose of all dynamic psychological theories, both in the wider area of depth psychology and in the more specialized area of social psychology, to study the psychic conflict. The symptoms of abnormal behavior especially in mental illness, have made investigators of human motivation aware that in many cases man is a divided man. His contradictory reactions, weakness and inability to adapt to the ordinary circumstances of family and social life have been general indications of the opposing forces which prevail in the human mind. Therefore the expression 'psychic' or 'psychological' *conflict* has come into use to sum up the dynamic problems of the human personality. All dynamic psychologists agree that man is in conflict. The particular problem which leads them to disagreements in theory and methodology is the search for the answer to the question: What is man in conflict with? To say that the psychic conflict is primarily an 'inner' fact of the human personality does not satisfy those who are studying man's subjective experiences in order to heal the troubled states created by those experiences. So, in order to answer the question of the nature and dimensions of the psychic conflict within the total life of the individual, various theories from all the fields of general anthropological research have been proposed. The philosophical and psychological theories aspire to give fixed answers, since their research lies more within the dimensions of subjectivity and the direct connections between this subjectivity and the values of life. On the other hand, the theories arising out of scientific depth psychological research are more directly related to philosophical inquiries which confront modern man's existential outlook in a dynamic way. Because of this connection which they have with the existential problems in the life of the individual, these theories prove useful to pastoral psychology in its attempt to understand the way in which the dynamic problem of the psychic conflict is conceived by modern psychology.

This study of the nature of the psychic conflict as conceived by depth psychology is a part of the more general effort of pastoral psychology to understand and present the outlines of this conflict in the setting of the total experience of human endeavor. At the core of even the simplest pastoral problem there is always a psychic conflict. Indeed where such a conflict is not found to exist there cannot be a pastoral problem. This basic principle in pastoral work makes it necessary to develop the material of pastoral psychology within the framework of the preconditions, structure and consequences of the psychic conflict.

INDIVIDUATION

The term 'individuation' has its origin in the psychological theory of the Swiss psychiatrist and psychologist Karl Gustav Jung. Jung uses the term to indicate deontologically the course of the psychic development of the individual. As we know, each individual's psychic development begins at the moment of his birth. He enters a process of psychological (and spiritual) maturation, the goal of which is to give maximum value to his human existence in all its dimensions. The individual *ought* to take the path which will lead to his full human development from every point of view.

Psychology is interested in following and studying the psychic development of the individual. But this basic aim of psychology is also of direct interest to all other anthropological dimensions, since the psychological basis for the development of the individual to wholeness is also a presupposition, or at any rate a concrete condition, for his general recognition as a human personality. For example, insofar as the philosophical study or psychiatric confrontation of the human person aims at a general understanding of him (for their field), they must also take into account the problems of the psychological substratum of the human person. Particularly in our time which, with its ideological, social political, technological and other 'symbols', underlines the problem of man's *total* existence, the psychological study of how one becomes a complete individual, and hence a 'full' human being, is essential for this overall understanding of him. Therefore before investigating the broader or higher existential links between the individual and the 'symbols' or 'values' of life, one should first have in view the picture of the process by which man becomes a psychologically complete human being. The particular branches of psychological science which are oriented at the same time towards an overall psychological understanding of the individual as he grows towards full psychological development endeavor to present this picture or to throw light on it.

To be sure, the term 'individuation' has more than a deontological character. That is, it not meant to refer only to the psychological purposefulness in the total life of the individual. It also defines the general framework of the psychological problem of development into a complete individual. Every person at birth starts on a journey of psychological development which *should* gradually make him a complete individual. But this psychological deontology obviously is not expressed at the same time as individual ontology. In other words, man's growth towards 'individuation' does not happen in the normal course of things and without hindrances. Therefore the term 'individuation' points as well to the many problems which can arise during this developmental process. The psychic development of the individual *should* move in an upward and forward direction. Various factors, however, create not only positive but also negative conditions along the way. Thus individuation has not only a deontological character ('should'), but also an ontological one. It conveys a hint of the practical biomatic problem involved in the attempt to reach the psychological goal of development to a 'full' individual.

FACTORS DETERMINING THE PROGRESS OF THE INDIVIDUAL TOWARDS PSYCHOLOGICAL FULFILMENT

The progress of the individual towards psychological fulfilment (individuation) always takes place within a concrete, *existential* framework. That is, the progress is not straightforward and self-evident. As we have said, it is determined by certain factors in the individual's 'being' which together constitute the basis or point of departure for the progress. These factors are well known and we shall simply recall them here.

a) *The psychological constitution.* Every individual is unique and unrepeatable with respect to the combination and intensity of his psychodynamic motives, which regulate his psychological behavior. The psychology of individual differences, in its attempt to study and propose a scientifically valid typology of human types and characters, comes up against the problem of the relativity of any such typology. This relativity is due to the absolute character of man's individual constitution.

The question of the 'inheritance' of behavioral motivation has a special place within the problem of the psychic constitution of the individual. This question is met chiefly in comparative studies of all the factors which ultimately determine behavior. Each individual is unique and unrepeatable, but in his uniqueness he is also the bearer of psychodynamic motives which stem from ancestral links in his ontogenetic chain, and also of motives arising from his *deepest* individual psychic identity. It is obvious, however, that we cannot draw a clear line between these two types of motivation. What can perhaps be recalled here is the fact that the motives which express structures of psychological behavior inherited from ancestral links are usually understood as factors which determine this behavior absolutely, while an ambivalent functional role is implied for the absolutely individual (not inherited) psychodynamic motives. It is rather the common conviction of many educators and psychologists, and more certainly of those concerned with the problems of education in a non-theoretical way, that the inherited characteristics of man's personality are difficult or even impossible to alter. Meanwhile it is regarded as self-evident that the uninherited (psychodynamic) characteristics are possible to influence in one way or another, positively or negatively (so they have an ambivalent character).

b) *The environment.* The natural and psychological framework within which the individual's psychic development takes place is made up of a broad synthesis of factors which influence or determine the nature and form of this process The natural environment the family, the social environment and the wider setting of the epoch contain a significant number of factors which *interfere* whith the basic progress of the individual towards psychic wholeness and determine it *irreversibly*. The types of effects which this great variety of environmental factors is likely to have upon the psychic development of the individual are the following. The environment may contribute:

1) to the normal and maximum development of individuality;

2) to a deviation, within the limits of 'normality,' of the course of this development, such that individuation does not approach its normal fullness, yet contributes to a satisfactory fulfilment of the aim of the individual as a human personality;

3) to blocking the way or even *stopping psychic development altogether at some stage.*

Almost all the psychological theories, and especially those of the school of depth psychology, are more concerned with the problems created by the second and third probabilities of the determinant relationship between the environment and the individual constitution. The first probability may not be utterly improbable, but it is not usual. The findings of depth psychology show convincingly that in the process of environmental influence (in any sense) the negative element usually comes out strongly, often playing a leading role in shaping the individual's psychic development. The positive element does not cease to be an object of psychological (mainly educational) investigation. Yet this positive element can be understood better through studying the negative, which is an immediate problem to the individual, since it interferes with his normal progress towards psychological maturity and fulfiment.

THE NEGATIVE FACTORS ON THE PATH TO PSYCHOLOGICAL FULFILMENT AS SOURCES OF INNER CONFLICT.

The deontological character of the individuation process suggests in the first place that the newborn child starts out with only positive and no negative elements as he begins his journey towards the gradual fulfilment of his psychological 'identity' (becoming what he *should* and *can* be). The common conception of the heredity-environment problem usually attributes responsibility for man's education or the shaping of character and behavior to the direct influence of the environment.[3] The idea which has already become almost absolute — not only in psychological theory but also in psychotherapeutic practice — that the focal point of the human problem must be in the 'first five years'[4] of life or in general in the 'traumatic experiences of childhood makes the environment responsible for subsequent psychic conflicts in the life of the individual. The analyst or psychotherapist, confronted with all the symptoms of any client's complex problems, will take care to refer back to his childhood experiences, and mainly the *negative* basic inner experiences. The sources of the psychic conflict, according not only to psychoanalysis but also to the theories of Adler and Jung, *must* be sought in childhood experiences.

This psychodynamic overempasis of the negative ('traumatic') environmental factors implies that conflicts are 'post-natal' in origin and consequently go back to the experiences which the individual had at the moment of birth and thereafter. Thus we arrive at the hypothesis that the environment into which the person is born and grows physically and mentally is *absolutely* responsible for the formation or generation of inner conflicts. This person is understood as the recipient of negative external influences which work together organically in 'setting up' the structure of his psychic conflict. For instance, a dictatorial father, and a mother (who may or may not be dictatorial as well), 'cooperate' in the *creation* and *development* of a psychic conflict in their child, whom they crush 'unpsychologically' in their effort to make a 'man' of him. Or parents who are in constant conflict (due to 'temperamental incompatibility') injure the psychic system of their child so deeply that, according to prevailing psychological theories and conceptions, they create in him the beginnings of an inner conflict, the symptoms of which will manifest themselves in later years.

But in spite of all this, this unsuspected overemphasis of the importance of the negative ('traumatic') factors in the environment may obscure *essential* sources of psychic conflict, which may lie in pre-natal psychic states. It does not occur to the analyst or psychotherapist to consider whether and to what extent any sources responsible for inner conflicts exist which are 'rooted' in the substantive nature of the psychic reality. The theories which the analyst or therapist have heard and respected have persuaded him that the psyche should be conceived more as a dynamic resultant of 'energies' than as a concrete 'substance.'

Freud condenses the concept of the psyche into the functioning of the *libido*, with a clearly mechanical and therefore indisputably materialistic character. Jung thinks in the same way basically, since he applies in an absolute way Busse's mechanistic-energic principles of *equivalence* and *constancy* to the relations between the conscious and the unconscious. According to Jung too the psyche functions exclusively as *energy*; it has no personal, substantive character; it is not an 'essence.' It simply shares in a wider psychic reality as a segment of that reality.[7]

These psychological theories which limit the nature of the human psyche in such an absolute way, confining the sources of psyche conflicts, as we have said, to 'post-natal' experiences and to situations in the life of the individual, leave untouched the question of whether these sources of conflict may extend beyond the environment into the area of individual psychic reality.

It is certainly true that with his always 'mechanistic' and 'materialistic' conception, Freud underlined the negativeness of the unconsious 'content.' But by his justification of this content Freud established it as a 'legal' psychic reality. For instance, the instincts and desires, according to Freud, are not subject to moral control or to the criticism of conscience. They are neither good nor bad. Moral evaluation of the contents of the unconscious is a result of interiorizing an external prohibition. For Freud the negative character of this interiorization makes the contents of the unconscious neutral with respect to moral evaluation. Thus the instincts and 'libidinous' desires which arise from the unconscious and seek expression and satisfaction in the conscious region do not characterize the 'psyche.' They simply express it. For this reason the analyst or psychotherapist who applies the principle of psychoanalysis cannot regard the content of the unconscious as a source of psychic conflict in the sense, let us say, of 'psychological' inferiority. The content of the unconscious has a 'right' to be expressed and to be satisfied (the *pleasure principle*). Psychological problems begin when external reality refuses to 'respect' the rights and demands of the unconscious (the *reality principle*).

Jung, with his notion of the collective unconscious, emphasized the fact that the 'psyche' in its basic structure (as a segment of the wider psychic reality) contains within it the 'purely) positive possibilities for man's true progress towards individuation. The 'archetypes' of the unconsious, as we shall see in the next chapter, are the crystalization and deposit of human experience and constitute the criterion for a sound solution to the problem of a psychic conflict. According to Jung, everyone is born with a collective heritage (i.e. common to all people without exception) of ways of behaving and of reacting to the stimuli and experiences of life in general. A person's entry into the process of an inner conflict takes place after his birth, that is, after the 'personal unconscious' is formed. Hence in the case of Jung's theory it is even clearer that he locates the sources of a psychic conflict in the post-natal experiences of the individual.

At this point it should be emphasized that pastoral psychology cannot accept that post-natal experiences are the only source of inner conflict, for it is a central thesis of Christian anthropology that every person at birth already carries the 'weight' of a psychic past. The concept of the sin of the forefathers, as accepted by Orthodox dogmatics, underlines the kind of decay and weakness with which the human psyche is already 'endowed' when the newborn individual is brought into field of interpersonal relations. Sin, not only as a spiritual concept but also as a psychodynamic fact, dominates and indeed 'operates' in the total life of the psyche. Ancestral sin, because of the universal extent and depth of its activity, 'seals' every human soul with such intensely corruptive and disruptive psychodynamic effects that the newly born person entering the realm of human relations already has within him the beginnings of the psychic conflict. Psychological theories see the environment, as the field in which the system of interpersonal relations unfolds (with the birth of the individual), to be place where a psychic conflict originally begins. But in the view of Christian anthropology the environment provides not the original causal factors of this conflict but the 'provocations,' the incitements and the 'spark' to set them off. Thus for pastoral psychology inner conflicts have their roots in the truly murky area of the human psyche, corrupted and weakened as it is by the corrosive effects of sin.

This thesis of pastoral psychology, clearly defined in the doctrinal teaching of Orthodox theology, gives broader dimensions to the problem of unconsious psychic reality which depth psychology vividly presents. For when the beginnings of the psychic conflict are sought in the depth of a human personality 'darkened' by the negative activities of sin, the problem of self-knowledge, with its maze-like complexity, includes all the hidden dimensions and aspects of the human psyche. It does not refer only to the system of interpersonal relations as stressed by most psychological theories (those of Adler, Jung, Fromm, V. Franklin K. Horney, etc.), but to man in his entirety as a monad as well as a member of a dyad or pleiad, and particularly in his connections with all the 'symbols,' values and experiences of life, in this world and beyond. In order for a person to learn *who he is*, it is not enough only to be aware of the nature and extent of each of his interpersonal relations. He must try to grasp the general picture in the light of his total connections with all the factors of his existence (God, the 'world,' the 'neighbor,' symbols, etc.). This picture, wider in dimensions and richer in psychodynamic 'shading,' reveals at the same time the broader dimensions of the psychic conflict. If this conflict is generally seen by psychology as man's conflict with himself and his 'neighbor,' for pastoral psychology it is his conflict with God as well.

ORIGINS AND STRUCTURE OF THE PSYCHIC CONFLICT ACCORDING TO THE BASIC PRINCIPLES OF MODERN PSYCHOLOGICAL THEORIES.

a) *The psychic conflict according to Freud's theory.*

Freud's 'topography' of the psyche distinguishes two fundamental psychic areas: the unconscious psychic life and the conscious psychic life. Freud's basic contribution to the establishing of depth psychology was the strong emphasis which his research and theories placed on the significance of the unconscious life for man's entire behavior and response to the external stimuli of life.

The unconscious inner life of man was not unknown territory *(terra incognita)* to the human mind in general before the time of Freud. Many philosophers much earlier than Freud had become aware of the unconscious realm of the psychic life, but no one else

had made such a determined effort to study it as Freud. Therefore
the impression was created that Freud had 'discovered' the unconscious and so had astonished the world just as much as Coper-
nicus. The observant human mind has never had any difficulty
in understanding many individual behavior responses as the results
of psychic motives which were hidden in an area that could not
be investigated as directly, for instance, as the reactions of the
senses.

Freud used the term *id* (it) to indicate the unconscious psychic
realm and the term *ego* (I) for the conscious realm which expresses
itself in a unified way and 'apparently' regulates man's entire
behavior. According to Freud, the unconscious is the source of instincts, desires and drives, which can be summed up in the term
libido. The libido is the basic instinctual drive of the unconscious
and is characterized as the pleasure drive, since its 'content' has
a hedonistic character. The psychic life, according to Freud, is set
in motion by the pleasure drive. In the first stage of the development of his theory Freud noted the opposition between this drive
and the *ego*, as it was clear that gratification of this drive was not
always unimpeded or possible. But since Freud was of the opinion
that his work on the 'neurotic' phenomenon could not be supported
by authoritative clinical findings, he then devised a third psychic
factor to solve the problem of the ego's refusal to obey the instinctive commands of the libido. If the individual does not gratify the
pleasure drive (libido), this means, in Freud's view, that some other
psychic factor is intervening between the id and the ego. He called this psychic factor the *superego*. The superego, Freud said, is
the censor which controls he circumstances under which the
pleasure drive 'shall' or 'shall not' be gratified.

Since, however, the 'shall' or 'shall not' is not derived from
the inner reality and structure of the psyche, this means that the
superego is an internalization of external prohibitions mainly due
to social, moral and other such conditions which govern and
regulate the social life. Thus, basically, psychic (instinctive) spon-
taneity conflicts with external reality, and this conflict is internaliz-
ed, with the result that the libido goes back, is repressed, into the
unconscious from which it sprang. For Freud the basic psychic
conflict is set up by the 'pleasure principle,' which obliges the libido

to seek gratification, and by the principle of external reality (the reality principle), which prohibits this gratification.

At a later stage in the development of his theory and after his discovery of the destructive instinct, he summed up the basic psychic conflict between what he considered the two fundamental counter-balancing instinctive forces in the psyche: the love instinct and the death instinct. *Eros* and death, pleasure and the destructive tendency (sadism) are two opposite psychic drives which are in conflict and so constitute the basic process in the psychic life.

The inner conflict, then, according to the general lines of Freudian theory, can be summed up in the opposition which man experiences between instinctive drives and external prohibitions. The external prohibitions are barriers which the instinctive impluses crash against. Then, without the individual's awareness, these impulses are repressed into the unconscious. They return to their source. This repression, however, creates a new 'situation' in the unconscious, for in Freud's view no instinctive impulse is removed from the psychic sphere, however strong the repression may be. The impluse repressed into the unconscious will either be sublimated ('transformed' into a different psychic content which will fulfill the aim and role which the repressed impluse has played) or it will become the basis for the formation of a psychic complex. In the first case, where the impluse is sublimated, no psychic problem is created, because the psychic pressure is released by a new 'creation.' In the second case, however, the complex forms the structure of a psychic conflict which will be manifested in neurotic symptoms. The neurotic symptoms will be a compensation for the psychic role formerly played by the repressed libidinous impluse. Thus in no case does the psychic conflict[10] remain 'hidden.' It is evidenced by the 'symptom' which replaces the function of the repressed impulse.

b) *The psychic conflict according to C. G. Jung*

Jung, too, sees the origin of the psychic conflict in a strong repression, but it is a repression of conscious experiences of the personality.

In many circumstances of a person's life, unpleasant and mentally intolerable situations are created. In these circumstances a psychologically mature person, that is one who has reached an advanced degree of individuation, is able to perceive the psychological consequences of these situations and so tries to adjust to them as painlessly as he can. In Jung's view this person avoids repressing unpleasant situations by trying to understand them. He accepts or rejects these situations after he has become fully aware of their existential dimensions and of the need to find the best possible way of meeting them (in terms of his psychic behavior).

Certainly, however, the average person is not psychologically mature. Therefore in everyday reality it is most likely that a person will respond to the unpleasant or intolerable situations which arise in his life by repressions. What one cannot bear, what one dislikes, what is 'shocking' is most often met by the psychological mechanism of repression.

But what happens when a person represses an unpleasant or intolerable experience? The most likely thing is that he psychologically represses ('swallows,' 'presses down,' thrusts') this experience into his unconcsious. But into what unconscious?

According to Jung, the unconscious psychic region of the personality has two zones. The deeper zone is the realm of the collective unconscious, and the upper one is that of the personal unconscious. Repression, as a psychological function, is an unconscious movement of the psyche. A person who represses anything is unaware of doing so. Repression is a result of the general functioning of the personality and may have many causes relating to the conscious life of the individual. But the individual does not realize what he represses nor how he does it. Otherwise one would speak of suppression. Suppression, as a psychological act, is a conscious rejection (e.g. I do not *want* to laugh and I restrain myself by an effort of overcoming the reflexes involved). Repression, on the other hand, is always an unconscious psychic movement, by which one puts the unpleasant or unbearable experience 'into storage' in the region of the personal unconscious.

This 'secret' storage of unpleasant experiences in the personal unconscious nevertheless still constitutes a psychological problem. The conflict in the individual's unconscious life is interiorized absolutely. That is to say, although in his subsequent conscious life the individual does not directly face the experience of the conflict (for example, a disagreement between a father and son, a quarrel between husband and wife, an oppresive relationship between a pupil and teacher), the inner world of this individual is in a 'civil war,' in a peculiar controversy whose unresolved knots will be characterized as a *complex*.

According to Jung, when an unpleasant experience, having become a 'content' of the psyche, is repressed into the personal unconscious, this means — by Busse's principles of 'equivalence' and 'constancy' — that a quantity of psychic energy from the conscious realm has been transferred (forcibly) to the unconscious. What psychic factor has brought about this forcible transfer (repression)? C. G. Jung replies: the *ego*, the centre of the conscious personality. Since the ego is the centre and regulator of the unity and identity of the psychic life and is the basic instrument by which the individual can adapt to external reality, it is this ego which does the repressing, but without knowing it! It consciously rejects the unpleasant experience and does not want to know it! It rejects it, avoids it in order to accomplish the 'forgetting' which will rid it of this intolerable burden. But since, on the basis of Busse's principles, every experience is still an inner experience and a psychic content, Jung's view is that dynamically no psychic content is removed from the psychic sphere (by repression). The ego continues to maintain its *organic* (genetic) relationship with the experience which it has repressed. Thus while an individual thinks that he has forgotten an unpleasant experience, the experience as a psychic phenomenon is sheltered in the personal unconscious and is still organically related to the psychic factor which repressed it, the ego.

As we have said, this organic relationship between the ego and the repressed content is maintained without the ego's knowledge. The ego (the individual) thinks that he is rid of the experience which has ceased to have a 'place' in his conscious life. However, just the opposite is the case. Jung's view is that by virtue of the unconscious character of repression the repressed experience has gained 'despotic' power over the ego. The ego by its basic hostile attitude has, as it thinks — or does not think, since the repression is an entirely unconscious act — broken off all *relations* with the unpleasant experience which had become intolerable. But this experience now holds the ego in its 'power.' This relationship between the ego and the repressed psychic content is characterized by Jung as 'identification with a complex.' This identification constitutes the structure of the conflict as Jung understands it.

The psychological consequences of this structure are, first, of all, that the psyche loses its inner freedom. Since the ego is ensnared in the complex activity of the repressed psychic content, it does not always act on its own 'volition' and 'thought' but by reflex carries out the orders 'despotically' imposed by this content. Every complex, as a product of repression, harasses the conscious psychic life whenever this life clashes with, or simply encounters, stimuli relating to the original experience of the conflict. (Cf. the popular saying: 'In the home of one who has been hanged one must not speak of a rope.')

Finally, what should be especially emphasized here is that as far as the content of the conflict is concerned, Jung accepts that it is usually connected with a moral problem.[11] All of the examples which Jung cites in his writings in order to throw light on the various aspects of the psychic conflict have to do with problems of conscience. Despite the fact that he himself is not interested in the axiological content of the concepts of 'conscience,' the 'moral person' or 'ethics,' he acknowledges that there is no psychic conflict without a moral (or religious) content. So he sees the structure of the conflict not as an entirely 'individual' problem (as in the case of Freud's theory), but as a problem certainly individual in the first place, but arising within the network of human relations. Man is in conflict with the 'other,' and he internalizes this conflict in an absolute way. That is, his problem does not remain the 'other' but becomes his conscience, which (as Jung agrees) plays a leading role in shaping the structure of the conflict.

c) *The psychic conflict according to A. Adler's theory.*

Adler too sees the genetic causes of the psychic conflict in man's outward life, in the enviroment. According to his view, man's basic goal is to have social recognition and an 'impact' in his human relationships. The psychic conflict arises within these conditions of man's life. Hence the structure of the inner conflict, in Adler's view, can easily be understood when one is familiar with the main lines of his theory which concern man's effort to reach his basic goal.

First of all, it is Adler's fundamental idea that a man's psychic life is determined by a goal. 'This goal emerges automatically from the demands of the organism and of the outer world, as well as from the response which the organism makes to it.'[12] Therefore 'it seems impossible to regard the psychic organ in any other way than as directed towards a goal, and individual psychology considers all the manifestations of the human soul as though they were directed towards a goal.' Therefore the individual always has before him a guideline which determines his course as he tries to realize the basic goal of his life. This line guides him to the attainment of power and authority in the social milieu (narrower and wider) in which he lives.

But, says Adler, 'Man, seen from the standpoint of nature, is an inferior organism.'[13] He lacks the capacities and powers which are always needed in order to achieve his goal smoothly and unimpeded. Nor does the social environment always offer the best conditions for this achievement. If a person is unable to realize his basic goal, his innate feeling of inferiority is intensified and obliges him to make a new effort in order to *compensate* or *balance* this feeling by seeking and discovering new partial goals. So he is led to the need to create a fictitious image of life and a fictitious goal. Insofar as this new effort brings satisfaction, his life goes forward, impelled by his feelings of inferiority, torwards the realization of his fictitious goal. But it may be that the feeling of inferiority becomes intensified,[14] and there is a danger that he will not be satisfied with a simple compensation for his anguish over greater 'social' failures. In this case he will go on to 'overcompensate' his painful feelings of inferiority with morbid anxiety reactions. Then he will find himself at the epicenter of a psychic crisis. He will live in a conflict between his weakness and the 'reactionary' forces of the enviroment.

In Adler's view too the psychic conflict is not usually experienced consciously. 'The pursuit of superiority over others,' he says, 'is not a manifest goal. The existence of a social feeling prevents its frank development. It must always grow in secret and hide itself behind a friendly mask.'[15] This means essentially that Adler too understands the unconscious psychological basis of the inner conflict within the general framework of depth psychology.

That is, the compensation or overcompensation of the feeling of inferiority is powered by strong repressions which create psychological 'complexes.' Thus here too the formation of the 'inferiority complex' is identified with the structure of the psychic conflict.

d) *The psychic conflict in the theory of K. Horney.*

Karen Horney also offers a theory of the psychic conflict which comes within the general lines of depth psychology.

Its basic thought has the same general dimensions as the other depth psychological theories. She sees the inner conflict as the most basic fact in man's life in all the dimensions of his existential outlook. 'A belief in a basic conflict within the human personality is ancient and plays a prominent role in various religions and philosophies. The powers of light and darkness, of God and the devil, of good and evil are some of the ways in which this belief has been expressed.'[16] Although she applied Freud's theory to a great extent, Horney was not convinced that his basic thought explained correctly the cause of the phenomenon of the psychic conflict. That is, she did not agree with the Freudian contention that 'the opposition between primitive egocentric drives and our forbidding conscience is the basic source of our manifold conflicts.'[17] For, as she found from her clinical experience, the result of the *basic psychic* conflict is so disastrous that it disrupts the life of the individual completely. Accordingly, the nature of the psychic conflict cannot be reduced to the narrow limits of an instinctive opposition within the psyche. For Freud the psychic conflict, as we have said, is inescapable. For Horney 'the basic neurotic conflict does not necessarily have to arise.'[18] It is possible for the individual to escape this conflict if he has had a sound upbringing and has a sound orientation in his relationships with other people. Therefore Horney sees the basic conflict as a disturbance in human relations. She too accentuates the social element in the life of the individual, saying: 'I see the basic conflict of the neurotic in the fundamentally contradictory attitudes he has acquired towards other persons.'[19] That is, the very desires or inclinations of the neurotic person go in opposite directions and so express the structure of the psychic conflict. 'As I see it,' says Horney, 'the source of the conflict revolves around the neurotic's loss of capacity to wish for anything whole-heartedly because his very wishes are divided, that is, go in opposite directions.'

With regard to the general pattern of the psychic conflict in Horney's theory, we should underline particularly the significance of the image which the individual forms of himself as the conflict develops. According to Horney, there are two main ways in which the individual tries to resolve his conflicts or to free himself from them. 'One of these consists in repressing certain aspects of the personality and bringing their opposites to the fore; the other is to put such distance between oneself and one's fellows that the conflicts are set out of operation. Both processes induce a feeling of unity that permits the individual to function, even if at considerable cost to himself.'[21] At the same time, these ways of reacting to the psychic pressure which is created within the individual by the basic inner conflict show the very deep nature of the conflict. They indicate that the individual is primarily in conflict with himself[22] and that the disturbance in his human relationships is a *projection* of this conflict upon those relationships. The fact that K. Horney understands the psychic conflict essentially as an inner split which is purely 'individual' in character is evident from the emphasis she gives to the 'idealized image' which the individual forms of himself in his effort to be released from the intolerable inner pressure which his conflict creates.

According to K. Horney, a further attempt on the part of the neurotic to be released from his conflict 'is the creation of an image of what the neurotic believes himself to be, or of what at the time he feels he can be or ought to be. Conscious or unconscious, the image is always in large degree removed from reality, though the influence it exerts on the person's life is very real indeed.'[23] The individual always remains unaware of this influence, since 'in all its essentials the idealized image is an unconscious phenomenon.' Thus in an unconscious way, the more removed from reality the neurotic individual perceives his self-image to be, the more 'it makes the person vulnerable and avid for outside affirmation and recognition.'[25] He becomes arrogant and is dominated by the conviction that he is perfect in every respect. Therefore 'the idealized image is a decided hindrance to growth, because it denies shortcomings or merely condemns them.' The idealized image, then, lacks the genuineness of authentic ideals. For, according to Horney, 'genuine ideals make for humility, the idealized image for arrogance.'[26]

Finally, according to Horney, the basic psychic conflict, as it is characteristically expressed in the lives of neurotic individuals, cannot be understood unless it is seen to depend organically on the moral[27] factor in general. She raises the same question before proceeding to develop the content of her book *Neurosis and Human Growth*. 'There is a wide divergence of opinion about the desirability or necessity of a disciplinary inner control system for the sake of insuring moral conduct . . . should we not, in accordance with the Christian injunction ("Be ye perfect . . . "), strive for perfection? Would it not be hazardous, indeed ruinous, to man's moral and social life to dispense with such dictates?"[28] Furthermore, she attributes the failure of her teacher, Freud, to evaluate correctly the role of conflicts in neurosis to the fact that Freud endeavored to develop a psychology free of moral values.

On the contrary, according to Horney, values and the cultural conventions of life play a basic role in creating or limiting[29] conflicts. For this reason, if one wanted to apply literally Freud's views on masochistic and sadistic impulses, which express the conflict between the constructive and destructive powers of human beings, moral values would have to be introduced here too. It is now understood that the inner conflict, in whatever area of a person's life it may be expressed, has a direct, organic connection with the specific factor in his life, and, more generally, with the moral values which he experiences positively or negatively. Horney is not a moralist, but she understands the basic psychic conflict in such a way as to present it ultimately as the individaul's antagonistic relationship to the cultural conditions and the social and moral conventions of his daily life.

   e) *The psychic conflict according to Igor Caruso's theory*

The goal of human existence, according to Caruso, is progressive personalization. This goal is analyzed in his book *Bios, Psyche, Person*[30] in such a way as to make plain the biological, social and axiological substratum of the dialectical course of personalization. Compared with Jung's term 'individuation,' it does seem that the term 'personalization' is richer in axiological elements. In the first place, there is an axiological difference between the terms 'person' and 'individual.'

The axiological difference between the terms 'individuation' and 'personalization' can be understood better if we look at Caruso's previous work in which he developed his theory of neurosis on the basis of the direct relationship between depth psychological findings and the values of life.[31]

According to Caruso, neurosis is a mental disorder which shows the kind of conflict in which man lives. He characterizes neurosis as man's negative, and at the same time positive, attempt to discover the way to find and restore 'life-orthodoxy.' For neurosis demonstrates the depth and breadth of a psychic conflict which is essentially 'existential' in character. 'Neurosis' says Caruso, 'has a deeply upsetting function in human destinies and also imposes upon them the obligation to new and positive action. Neurosis is both a betrayal of what we are called to be in life and a confirmation of that calling.'[32] This means that neurosis (in its negative aspect) is an 'apostasy,' a 'life-heresy.' But it comes of an *erring conscience.* 'Erring though the conscience may be, it is still a conscience.' Neurosis has a positive character as well. 'Neurosis is not merely a lie, it is also in some way the sensitive conscience's patent of nobility.'[33]

So, according to Caruso, neurosis is both falsehood and truth at the same time. Within the neurotic structure the erring conscience (caused by the person's rejection of the hierarchy of values) functions effectively, but so does the sensitivity of the healthy conscience. The person is ultimately in conflict with his conscience. He violates it and establishes this violation as an absolute value in his life. At the same time he suffers, however, for while he perceives the violation of his conscience as a 'life-heresy' and understands its untruth, he cannot 'existentially' approach the truth which this lie denies. Therefore 'each neurotic phenomenon must be regarded as being positive and negative *at the same time*; for there occurs the struggle between good and evil, yea and nay, truth and lie in each neurotic phenomenon. The tragic destiny of existence, weary of its own limitations and for ever trying to bridge the paradox of wanting to participate simultaneously in being and non-being, is reflected in neurosis.'[34]

So the basic meaning of the psychic conflict which is expressed by neurosis, the 'typical' and 'representative' disease of our time, is a moral one. Since neurosis is a vital manifestation, it cannot be understood otherwise than as a conflict between the individual and his conscience. According to Caruso, psychology has itself become neurotic because it is identified with the character of neurosis. Neurosis is the absolutization of the relative. Psychology absolutizes the data of the individual's earthly life and denies the moral character of that life. But moral neutrality in judging a phenomenon which is itself caused by a defection from the concept of value, is an impossibility.'[35] Therefore neurosis has a deeply moral meaning, which springs from its inescapable dependence on the conscience, but also on the universal hierarchy of values. The latter means that neurosis has a wider moral character, which underlines its 'existential' significance for the person. For in the course of developing a neurosis the individual is not facing an unimportant or secondary problem in his life but a truly 'existential' problem, which (as a neurotic phenomenon) may prove to be a 'sickness unto death.' Finally neurosis is the critical position of a person faced with life and death. In the psychological and axiological dynamics of the neurotic process, as Caruso says, the 'yea' and the 'nay' of life, the 'to be' and 'not to be' are at stake.

GENERAL CONCLUSIONS

The statement of the basic lines of the main psychological theories about the origins and structure of the psychic conflict shows the problems to which the search for a valid theory adequate to the nature of the human personality leads. Everyone who introduces a specific psychological theory connected with the basic psychic conflict tries to make it convincing by giving a *universal* account of man's many sided functions. Even Freud, who wanted to keep to the instinctive dynamics of the human personality, did not refrain from applying his naturalistic theory to the whole picture of the personality. Since then all the other representatives of depth psychology have more and more readily overstepped the limits of scientific psychologism, making this psychologism absolute for the whole of human existence. Nevertheless a critical look at the variety of psychological positions taken with regard to the psychic conflict makes it possible to find out *deductively* which dynamic elements in the human personality are emphasized by each. This knowledge is useful to pastoral psychology, which, because of the nature of its work and its missions, aims to study the phenomenon of the psychic conflict from many sides. The question of which dynamic elements in the human personality, or which of its existential connections are highlighted in each psychological theory having its own picture of the psychic conflict, leads us to an extremely interesting answer, which we must scrutinize before we can approach the problem of this conflict in the framework of pastoral psychology. With this in mind, let us recall the main elements of each psychological theory which projects the structure of the psychic conflict as that theory understands it.

a) Freud's theory raises the instinctive dynamism of the unconscious realm to the position of a vital dialectical relationship of opposites (Eros and Death).

b) Jung's theory brings out the antithetical powers of the psyche which, in their total opposition, express the need for integration (individuation). He understands the psychic conflict as a tendency towards the uniting of opposites (*compositio oppositorum*), but he also sees the 'moral' character of this conflict. The psychic is a state in which the individual lacks inner freedom, due to his failure to understand his 'shadow' and so to make a sound 'moral' choice (compatible with the demands of the collective unconscious).

c) Adler's theory emphasizes the vital importance of the social factor for the individual. Man is in pursuit of a basic goal. This goal is social recognition. But the graph of a person's life is drawn in a process of conflict between his feeling of inferiority and his need for social recognition. Finally, man is in constant conflict with social feeling.

d) K. Horney's theory emphasizes the significance of human relations in the origin and structure of the inner conflict. In the first place the individual is in conflict with other people. But this conflict ultimately develops into a conflict with himself. Horney gives special emphasis to the organic correlation of the values of life with the psychological problems of the individual. Without this organic correlation we could not, in her view, understand the nature and dimensions of man's innner conflict.

e) Caruso's theory lays more stress on the moral character of the inner conflict. He understands this conflict as result of a failure to achieve personalization. The inner conflict is mainly a conflict with one's conscience. At the same time this conflict reveals man's moral sensitivity and therefore also expresses an effort to return to 'life orthodoxy,' that is to moral order and balance in life.

Thus the different 'projections' of depth psychology endeavour to throw light of the following aspects of the human psyche which is in conflict with itself:

a) On its instinctive element (Freud)
b) On its antithetical inner functioning (Jung)
c) On its social dynamic character (Adler)
d) On the axiological dynamics of human relations (Horney)
e) On the moral dynamism of conscience (Caruso).[36]

If we leave aside the absolutizations to which, as we have said, the different psychological theories resort as a rule in order to justify themselves, the accentuation of these aspects of the inner conflict can lead to a *synthesis* which will throw light on this basic phenomenon in human existence. In each case the one-sidedness of the investigation and at the same time the absolutizing of this one-sidedness are due to the interest which the proponent of each theory has in the 'scientific' justification of his theory. But to examine the psychic conflict in the framework of man's existence in general is in the interest of the truth. For this reason we must appreciate the usefulness and validity of the knowledge offered us by the psychological theories which we have seen, but at the same time 'critically' determine the degree and type of their inadequacy (because of the one-sided investigations). Pastoral psychology accepts the validity of this knoweledge and determines the extent of its usefulness in each case on the basis of an objective understanding of its insuficiency.

CHAPTER TWO

THE STRUCTURE OF
THE BASIC PSYCHIC CONFLICT

THE OVERALL PICTURE OF THE FINDINGS
OF DEPTH PSYCHOLOGY

Before sketching the main structure of the psychic conflict as understood by pastoral psychology within the anthropological teaching of Orthodox theology, it will be useful to get a unified picture of the various findings of depth psychology which throw light on the particular aspects of the conflict. According to these findings the basic structure of the inner conflict can be put together into the following psychodynamic scheme.

As to the origin of the inner conflict, it seems that the depth psychological findings permit us to stress the fundamental role played by certain central psychodynamic factors which are correlated in a *dialectical* process of existential dimensions. That is, the spirit of these findings indicates that the inner conflict is not a purely endopsychic occurrence but is always organically and dynamically related to basic factors in human existence and life. These are the *biomatic, axiological* and *social* factors. In their dialectic correlation, these three central pscyhodynamic factors in each particular individual make up a concrete image of the 'existential outlook' of this personality. That is, by their functional dynamic relationship these factors lead the individual to form a *basic* image of life which dominates his whole existence. This 'existential outlook' is the picture which the individual has before him (consciously or unconsciously), to which he strives to conform (whether he is aware of it or not).

a) *The biomatic factor in the basic structure of the psychic conflict*

The expression 'biomatic factor' is used here synoptically to mean the given psychodynamic disposition or constitution of the individual. According to the synthetic picture of the findings of depth psychology, man begins his life with an existential obligation: to develop or unfold into a specific psychodynamic type of individual (individuation) or 'person' (personalization). He certainly cannot be understood apart from the pursuit of some basic goal (Adler). This goal, as V. Frankl (Logotherapy) has shown in detail, underlines every person's need for a meaning in life. This indicates that the biomatic factor (even in the Freudian sense) is necessarily associated with a concrete purposiveness. The psychodynamic set or the psychosomatic constitution of the individual is not to be understood statically but dynamically and operatively as *movement* towards the realization of a goal.

b) *The axiological factor in the basic structure of psychic conflict.*

The axiological factor functions as general command which compels the individual to choose between the demands of the *biomatic* or *social* factor and the *values* in life. The fact that Freud admitted the necessity of this choice even if it was under the pressure of instinctive processes (a conflict between the pleasure principle and the reality principle) shows that it is in the nature of the psychic conflict either to move towards fulfilling the (positive) choice or to 'perpetuate' an unfortunate choice. As Caruso said, neurosis, which best expresses the existential character of the psychic conflict, is a person's effort to utter a 'yea' or a 'nay,' or else it is his living of an unfortunate choice made between the 'yea' and the 'nay.' The overall spirit of the findings of depth psychology underlines particularly the axiological content of this affirmation and negation. The 'yea' and the 'nay' refer to respect for the hierarchy of values. The inner conflict is the encounter of opposites which have axiological significance for the human personality.

c) *The social factor in the basic structure of the psychic conflict.*

The biomatic and hence also the axiological sphere of existence

within which the individual acts, moves, expresses himself and functions as a self-existing personality is the social sphere. This fact
of the social character of the life of the individual also determines
the social character of the psychic conflict. According to Erich
Fromm, Freud basically saw the individual in isolation from the
social whole, as a human monad, related to the 'other' only in connection with satisfying libidinous needs. Even in Freud's case,
however, the reality principle establishes an organic link between
the social factor in general and the problems of the psychic conflict.

Adler in particular emphasized social feeling and the
significance of the social sphere in the origin and development
of the psychic conflict. K. Horney convincingly analyzed the unconscious processes which lie hidden beneath the surface of the
intricate social relations of the individual.

The psychodynamic result of the three factors in the basic structure of the psychic conflict is expressed in the 'existential outlook.'
As we have said, this outlook is the image which the individual
has before him (consciously or unconsciously) and to which he is
required ('commanded' by an inner necessity) to conform. This
command to conform (especially as an unconscious function) is a
purposiveness which is beyond the bounds of rational consciousness
and so can be repressed, but it is never definitively and irrevocably
done away with. Thus the dynamic 'content' of the inner conflict
is reflected in the individual's attainments with respect to his basic
goal, in his ideals and in his axiological pursuits in general. The
quality of the 'existential outlook' is better shown, however, in the
individual's failures in his effort to become what he should be.
Depth psychology, with its research into the unconscious substratum
of the human personality, investigates precisely not only the way
in which the individual tries to achieve self-realization, but also
the quality of his 'existential outlook'. Yet within these dimensions
of human existence it is in fact exploring the nature and character
of the psychic conflict. This means that the different schools of
depth psychology study this basic phenomenon in the psychic life
from all sides. Nevertheless, from whichever side one examines
the inner conflict through the data of depth psychology, it will be
understood in the end that the total picture of these findings leads
naturally to the field of pastoral psychology. For the structure of
the basic conflict which we find in this picture can likewise be found

outlined in the anthropological teaching of Orthodox theology. This
further justifies not only the use of certain findings of depth
psychology by pastoral psychology, but also the study of he basic
psychic conflict from the point of view of psychological or pastoral
theological connections.

Finally, the special reason for bringing depth psychology and
pastoral psychology to a *common* examination of such a fundamental human problem as the psychic conflict is the *synthetic*, indeed
organic, character of the interrelationship of the three
psychodynamic factors in the conflict. To isolate each factor and
examine its role in the origin and development of the psychic conflict is artificial. It is a methodological necessity which permits
us to understand the details as well as the whole. But this understanding is fragmentary if we stop at this artificial separation of
the three psychodynamic factors in the inner conflict. The human
'person' cannot be understood by the method of 'particular' examinations. In combination with the particular, partial examinations it is also necessary to take into account the indissoluble
organic cohesion of the psychodynamic functions which are expressed in the total picture of human existence and life. Seen from
this point of view (that the process of the psychic conflict cannot
be analyzed into 'self-existent' psychodynamic factors), the human
personality compels pastoral psychology to investigate the
phenomenon of the inner conflict in the sphere of Christian anthropology, referring at the same time to those findings of depth
psychology which can also be confirmed by the basic picture of
this anthropology. Therefore we shall proceed to examine the structure of the basic psychic conflict according to the relevant material
in Holy Scripture.

THE STRUCTURE OF THE PSYCHIC CONFLICT ACCORDING TO
THE OLD TESTAMENT NARRATIVE CONCERNING MAN
(Gen 2.15-3,19)

In the Old Testament story which describes man's creation by
God and his temptation and fall, we have the outline of the primordial structure of the psychic conflict, which has been the basic
characteristic of the human personality ever since.

As we know, the beginning of human life is indelibly marked

by a *commandment*. Man's life as personal and free activity 'had to' have an 'existential' starting point which would make it possible, from the very first moment of his self-awareness, to function as *moral* and *spiritual* nature. This starting point was God's command: 'And the Lord God commanded the man, saying, "From every tree of the garden you may freely eat; but from the tree of the knowledge of good and evil you shall not eat, for in the day that you eat the fruit of it you shall surely die" ' (Gen 2. 16-17). Man's life begins with a 'compulsory' (commanded') act of choice. He is called to choose between two mutually contradictory 'necessities' which together confirm his freedom. That is, by the very fact that man is able to choose one or the other he is shown to be free, and this freedom must be lived and expressed by his response to the command. Either he must remain an 'individual'[1] on his own, 'subject' to an absolute egoistic necessity to function individually, or he must remain a partaker of the divine nature and advance this participation to an experience of 'divine likeness': he must become 'God by grace,' 'subject' to the will of God. Thus with his first step in life man enters the existential arena of the psychic conflict. This means that before his fall into sin this conflict is already established as an affirmation and confirmation of his freedom to make his own decisions and to choose the 'paths' of his existential outlook. The psychic conflict before the fall is understood as not only the *highest* but also the *universal* spiritual functioning of human nature. Without this the human personality cannot function as an 'image of God,' an image intended also to be transformed into the experience of the 'likeness' of God.

Before the fall, then, motivation of life had a positive character with a counterbalancing flow. This way of life is characterized as a 'psychic conflict' because it is understood as such by the spirit of fallen man, who finds himself caught up in this psychospiritual vicious circle in his experience of life.[2] But before the fall, since man did not yet have the experience of decay and death, the psychic conflict which had been set in motion by God's commandment simply had the character of the inner conflict and its destructive consequences highest and universal functioning of the human personality. After the fall man became aware of the negative character of the inner conflict and its destructive consequences for his psychosomatic integrity.

So God's commandment leads man into a process of 'psychic conflict' which is essentially a process of *choice*[3] This process when completed will have one of two results. Either man will overcome his egoistic motives, transcending them in order to submit to the will of God, or he will become their slave, out of 'individual' self-interest. In the first case the psychic conflict will terminate simultaneously with its positive outcome. Man's 'servitude' or 'subjection' to the will of God will complete his freedom and stabilize it permanently. In the second case the psychic conflict will continue to be the basic psychospiritual function of the human personality, since man's worldly success in becoming an 'individual' through the fall will fix more permanently his inner dividedness into two opposing desires and dispositions, as the Apostle Paul epigrammatically crystallized this split, in his seventh chapter to the Romans, which is classic for our situation.

We are already in the reality of the second result of the *dramatic* choice of the first man, and now, after the fall, we understand human life as an ongoing psychic conflict. Indeed this process is described not only with great clarity, but with generality at the same time, in the lines of the text which follow the definition of the content of God's command. With very expressive simplicity the writer of this text gives us the primordial structure of the psychic conflict as it was experienced by the first man. The correlation of this structure with the psychic conflict which is characterized in our time as 'neurosis' leads us to the conclusion — obvious in any case — that since the fall the inner conflict has remained the basic psychospiritual function of man's personality. Just as Adam experienced inner conflict, so this conflict is still experienced by the Christian who, as a member of the body of the Church of Christ, strives conscientiously to become 'conformed to his image.' The differences which can be found between the primordial structure of the psychic conflict and that of the conflict after the fall do not affect the basic picture of it as formed by the process of *choice*. Even within the life of the Church, as we shall see, the inner conflict still maintains its original distinctive characteristics. The only difference in this case is that the prospect of resolving the conflict, as a *possibility* and a *reality*, is altered. Otherwise the Christian as a member of the Body of Christ still experiences *opposing* inner states, which always express the primordial structure of the psychic conflict. For these latter reasons we must take a more detailed look at the outline of the basic psychological conflict as the Old Testament gives it to us.

a) *The existential outlook of the Adamic couple (the 'likeness')*
The Adamic couple was created within a *definite* existential perspective. The divine thought: 'Let us make man in our image, according to our likeness; let them have dominion over the fish of the sea, over the birds of the air, and over the cattle, over all the earth and over every creeping thing that creeps on the earth' (Gen 1.26) defines *a priori* the existential outlook of the Adamic couple. This means that the first man was created within concrete existential dimensions. His existence would fulfil the purpose for which he was created.

The *a priori* definition of man's existential perspective underlines clearly that what a man *must* become exists potentially within his nature. The Fathers of the Church understood the 'image' as a dynamic beginning of the realization of the 'likeness.' The latter was to be made a living reality through the active unfolding of the 'image' within the sphere of existence. Thus man was created by God to pursue an appointed aim, which was the 'likeness.' He therefore has a definite existential entelechy in his nature. He must become what he can become, or he can become what he must become.

Apart from this basic element in human existence, we must also emphasize here the *authoritative* and *social* elements which are included in the divine thought and which define the two essential poles of man's course within the dimensions of his existential perspective. In the existential framework of the 'likeness' the authoritative element, in combination with the social, underline the indivisible interwovenness of the biomatic, axiological and social factors in human nature and lead us to the inescapable understanding that man is 'commanded' to realize the goal of his existence by means of a sovereign authority within the social sphere. This means that the 'likeness' will be realizable only if man's potentiality for *authority* within the social sphere functions in full growth.

In the picture which we have before us this authority is not to be understood as legal and administrative. Man was not born to dominate and govern. He was born to actualize the highest aim of the 'likeness.' This aim could be realized, however, only if a strong sense of his own dignity was at work in him. Since the fall this sense of dignity has in fact been characterized as 'egoism' or pride. Nevertheless we must recognize a healthy egoism before the fall as an essential instrument for realizing the 'likeness.' If at the beginning man had not been in a position to understand the highest aim of his existence or had not been psychodynamically motivated towards the 'likeness,' how could he have been asked to strip for a struggle — always toilsome and won through 'conflicts' — to realize the 'likeness'!

Summing up the basic dimensions of man's existential prospect, we would underline the organic, functional relationship which existed between man's sense of sovereign dignity and the social field in which the 'likeness' had to be realized. In other words, man was created by God to become like him, 'God by grace.' In order to be able to realize this aim of his existence, man was equipped with the psychodynamic motives necessary or appropriate to the nature of the aim. In the blessing which God gave after creating the Adamic couple, the element of authority ('have dominion') over nature, the 'creative' element ('be fruitful and multiply') and the 'sovereign' element ('fill the earth and subdue it') refer clearly to the divine plan (Gen 1.28). These elements together constitute the psychodynamic setting of the sense of ('divine') dignity which man had before the fall. He was born to become 'God by grace' and could become so. Not only did he become fully aware of this fact as he found himself face to face with God's command, but also he willed and desired it. This impetus towards 'likeness' is a special divine blessing bestowed upon man. According to the Fathers of the Church, this impetus is a recognition of the *religious* nature of the human personality and certifies the authenticity of his divine origin.

b) *Living by God's commandment (Gen 2. 16-17) as a 'temptation' and abuse of man's sense of dignity.*

The Adamic couple's vision of life changed significantly at the

moment when they found themselves faced with God's commandment, which defined more clearly (and more 'narrowly') the framework of their existential prospect. The command did not deny the
existential prospect (the 'likeness') but defined the path by which
the Adamic couple were to realize it. So it was the 'narrow' way
which lay before the couple, a way of 'prohibition'[4] and 'restric-
tion'! But this fact did not alter the first couple's vision of life,
because the command simply defined the 'way' towards realization of the 'likeness.' The change in the couple's vision of life was
brought about by the serpent's 'intervention' in their dialogue with
God's commandment. The way of the commandment did not
develop as man's own individual affair. He did not stand alone
before the commandment. At the 'entrance' to the 'way' stood the
serpent with much patience and 'subtlety' ('he was more cunning
than any beast of the field which the Lord God had made' — Gen
3.1). What role was the serpent to play in this situation which was
simultaneously opportune and critical for man?

The serpent's aim would be to urge man to reach the 'likeness'
in a shorter time. In this way the serpent would be responding
to man's legitimate longing for 'deification.' Thus began a dialogue
with an element of 'deceit' and 'falsehood.' The serpent said to
the woman, 'Has God indeed said, "You shall not eat from every
tree of the garden"?' He generalized the *prohibitive* element in
the commandment in order to call man's attention to the aspect
of the command which at first sight limited the possibilities of his
freedom. The woman corrected the serpent's 'lie' and repeated
correctly the content of the commandment. This served the purpose of the serpent, who took up only the last words of the command, in order to misrepresent God and supposedly prove man's
existential prospect to be mistaken. 'And the serpent said to the
woman, "You will not surely die. For God knows that in the day
you eat it your eyes will be opened, and you will be like God, knowing good and evil" '(Gen 3.4-5). This intervention by the serpent
in man's living the way of the commandment is usually characterized as a 'temptation.' For the serpent acted with partiality.
He incited those psychodynamic motives which ran directly counter
to the 'prohibition,' as well as those which were immediately and
organically connected with the aim to be achieved. It is true that

prohibitions always arouse 'negative' feelings, whereas any freedom
granted enhances the sense of human dignity. At any rate, the serpent facilitated man's entry into a psychic conflict which distorted
his existential perspective and so led him into error. For while the
serpent's lie satisfied man's sense of dignity and gave hope to his
longing for deification, it led him into the path of the 'demonic,'
which would actually bring him to his own self-deification (*homo
homini Deus*). This way is the reverse of the path of authentic
deification, which was defined by the prohibitive aspect of the
commandment.

The prohibition contained in God's command was for the purpose of granting human freedom and especially a sense of dignity. Without the intervention of the serpent the 'psychic conflict'
would have had a different character. With the intervention of the
serpent the 'demonic' element became a particular dimension in
the process of this conflict. Later, moreover in the Christian setting, these wise words of the Apostle Paul would be heard: 'We
do not wrestle against flesh and blood, but against principalities,
against powers, against the rulers of the darkness of this age, against
spiritual hosts of wickedness in the heavenly places' (Eph 6.12).
The demonic element slipped into the process of man's conflict
with his axiological inclinations in order to 'tempt' him and induce him to make a choice contrary to the existential prospect which
God had specified as the 'likeness.' In acting in conformity with
the demonic prompting, man acted with freedom, but this was the
freedom which God had given him so that he might be worthy of
his divine origin. Since the compliance with the demonic suggestion led to a functional perversion of the psychodynamic motives
of the human personality, which put an end to the inner discipline
of these motives and lost him his freedom, man's act of yielding
to the temptation meant a misuse of his freedom. Therefore it is
very true to say that the Adamic couple misused the freedom which
God had given them to enable them to express the orientation of
their values.

But one must not stop here. Man's misuse of freedom is often
emphasized at the expense of another, equally important misuse
by man: his misuse of the sense of his (divine) dignity. In his haste
to become 'God,' man accepted the services of the serpent in order

to succeed in this aim. So this holy and sacred motive of dignity was changed into a 'demonic,' egoistic element. It became a function of arrogance! Somehow even his own nature could not bear this misuse. That is why the psychic conflict since the fall of man usually makes its appearance with the most destructive, egoistic and arrogant motive of the human personality. Since the fall the psychic conflict has been experienced as an intolerable testimony of opposing egoistic impulses in the personality.[5] Man's egoistic impulses conflict with one another in such an uncontrollable 'mania' that (in the pastoral problems which one encounters, for instance) one sees the demonic character of an inconceivable disaster. The intensely egoistic individual who has any sort of psychic conflict finds himself on a course of self-destruction which he cannot understand and hence cannot control or overcome. The consequences of the fall as they unfold in the scriptural text make us understand this.

c) *Living with a wounded sense of dignity*

The first basic consequence of the transgression of God's commandment by the Adamic couple was that they became aware of a general inferiority of their outward (bodily) image. 'Then the eyes of both of them were opened, and they knew that they were naked; and they sewed fig leaves together and made themselves coverings' (Gen 3.7). The result of having chosen 'deification' through the intervention of the serpent was that the transgressors became aware of a nakedness which they themselves could not accept. Their effort to 'hide' this nakedness was due to the wounding of their sense of dignity. To be naked was a negative, unpleasant and unacceptable experience. This shows that the psychodynamic motivation of divine dignity which the transgressors of the commandment misused was activated to play a negative role: to conceal the wounding of man's 'divine image.' This effect upon the human personality as the first reaction after the fall underlines the primary meaning of the new egoistic psychodynamic functions in the psychic conflict. Hereafter the ego motives would play only a negative role. They would work to conceal the nakedness of the human 'face' and so to promote his 'individualistic' 'deification.'

But the negative dynamism of fallen man's egoistic motivation can be understood better if these motives are seen in connection with the existential prospect as defined by God in his creative design, the 'likeness.' The transgression of God's command did not lead the transgressors to the fullness promised by the serpent's suggestion. Man's longing for deification remained unfulfilled and this was certainly shown clearly by the reaction of the Adamic couple on becoming aware of their nakedness. If we did not have such a reaction we could accept that the transgression of the commandment transferred the Adamic couple to a *status quo* that was neutral in value orientation, to an axiological indifference towards the existential prospect appointed by God. But man's reaction, the feeling of inferiority which his failure to realize the 'likeness' created in him, shows that this failure was at the same time a negative functioning of his divine dignity, which continued to seek the 'likeness' even in this state of fallenness and failure. The same self-respect which had been wounded was working, even if in a negative way, to save what it could from the ruins of the human 'face.'

Perhaps at this point it is possible to confirm the findings of depth psychology and psychotherapy that in human life there are two 'visions' of the existential prospect. One is genuine and ideal and marks a life of existential wholeness, psychospiritual integration and happiness. The other is an 'idealized image' (K. Horney): to live by such an image exhibits the dimensions of a perpetual inner conflict and means psychospiritual inferiority, immaturity, adversity and unhappiness for the individual. The distinction between these two 'existential perspectives' shows, finally, that the fall inevitably established the psychic conflict in the form of a splitting of man into two contradictory perspectives. Motivated by a distant (but 'saving') inner echoing of the 'likeness,' fallen man tries to live by the idealized image which his wounded self-respect sets before him. A call to perfection deposited very deep within him remains as a motivation of his 'neurotic' need for perfection.[6] This fact reveals the most fundamental aspect of the human drama which is set forth in Genesis 3.7 with such astonishing simplicity but also unimaginable existential depth. After the fall man would try to hide his 'nakedness,' with the 'best robe' (Lk 15.22) before the eyes of his unconscious. But in every case this would also be the deepest meaning of man's inner conflict, his endless torment!

d) *The structure of the basic psychic conflict as the 'Adam complex'*

We have come now to a second phase in the development of the structure of the psychic conflict. This is the phase of Adamic man's reaction towards himself. In Genesis 3.8-13 we have fallen man's reaction to the consequences to himself of having transgressed God's commandment, and finally we have his reaction towards *himself.* These reactions express all the dimensions of the basic structure of the inner conflict and reveal the way in which fallen man experiences and 'projects' this conflict.

In the eighth verse the biblical text presents God calling for an explanation from the transgressor of his commandment. The 'Adamic man' felt God's presence very near at a certain moment and proceeded to react in a certain way. 'And they heard the sound of the Lord God walking in the garden in the cool of the day, and Adam and his wife hid themselves from the presence of the Lord God among the trees of the garden.'

The nearness of God's presence and movement arouses a primary reaction in the Adamic couple: *flight* by the particular behavior of 'hiding' 'among the trees of the garden.' This very fact shows that the situation created by the transgression was unacceptable even to the transgressor himself. For the transgression not only did no honour to his self-respect, but, as we have said, it wounded it. So a state of psychic inferiority resulted, any reminder of which still causes 'fallen' man to flee far from the 'recollection' of the circumstances which gave rise to it. Anything that reminds the transgressor of his transgression is undesirable and must be kept at a distance.

At this point we must mention the difficulties which would be encountered by an interpreter who wished to make use of the whole text of Genesis concerning the creation and fall of man in order to define precisely the anthropological, psychological, moral, social and other dimensions of man's life. However, without denying the real presence of God in the development of the human drama with the directness in which this text presents it, it must be said that this external picture of the dialogue of God with the transgressor can also be seen in a different light, that of the interiorization of an external authority now represented and functioning through man's conscience. The closeness of God's presence ('they *heard* the *sound* of the Lord God . . .') can mean both, that is, the real presence of God and at the same time the functioning of the 'wounded' conscience of the transgressor, the Adamic man. The whole picture of the creation and fall of man, as we know, is strongly anthropomorphic in character with respect to the presence and actions of God. But this anthropomorphism is valid in our case when seen in terms of the conscience. The one fact cannot exclude the other. Probably the biblical picture is intended also to allude to the functioning of the conscience, which is in a position to 'hear' the voice of God, or which God is able to make his own voice.

What must be seen here in any case is that the picture we have before us certainly aims to present the creative work of God and his connection with the history of man in general, while at the same time it aims to allude to the inner processes set in motion by the transgression of God's commandment. So man's hiding can be understood also as a *flight* from his own awareness, from himself. Finally, it can be noted that since man was cut off from his communion with God by transgressing God's command, he became estranged from himself as well. Accordingly, the 'hiding' behind the trees of paradise is at the same time also man's hiding in his own 'shadow' behind himself!

In psychological terms this hiding means that man represses himself into his unconscious mind; and here too we can grasp the psychological meaning of the eighth verse if we combine the reaction which it describes with the spirit of the findings of depth psychology. Of course this 'primary' repression is stated clearly in the preceding verse. The 'hiding' of his nakedness is an image of the repression done by the transgressor. Disappointed at the result of his act, he quickly concealed this result, which was manifested by his nakedness. But certainly the eighth verse presents the reaction of repression more clearly. In the face of a disclosure of their transgression of God's command, the Adamic couple made haste to 'hide.' What psychodynamic factor motivated this repression? The next two verses explain the mental state of the transgressor simply and clearly and point to 'fear' as the basic motive for man's 'secondary' repression of himself.

'Then the Lord God called to Adam and said to him, "Where are you?" (verse 9). God's question was certainly asking what the transgressor's state was. His aim was to help him to reach a certain degree of self-awareness which would permit him to talk with God in the best way, that is, as constructively as it was possible for the Adamic man ruined by sin. God, who is love, was aiming to give man essential help for understanding the tragic situation into which he had fallen through yielding to the demonic suggestion. Therefore God's calling to Adam to reveal himself also has the positive element of making him aware, with the aim of bringing him back to face himself. And Adam did *reveal* himself. He told his reactions along with the basic psychodynamic motive which aroused them. 'So he said, "I heard your voice in the garden, and I was afraid because I was naked; and I hid myself" ' (verse 10). He confessed that fear had led him to the basic reaction of *flight* and *concealment*.

The problem posed by the tenth verse is: What can be the concrete starting-point of the fear in the whole system of the inner conflict of the Adamic man? Of course the easiest answer is punishment. Fear of the punishment which had been announced is the most reasonable explanation for the reaction of the man who was quick to hide himself. But if we recognized it as permissible here too to associate Adam's fear with the spirit of the depth psychological theory of neurosis, we could more easily understand that this fear had more to do with his repressed self than with the threat of punishment. We can comprehend this also apart from that association, as man's fear of himself, as far as we understand the extensive damage done to his psychospiritual nature by sin. The Adamic transgressor was in the first place afraid of himself as he now saw himself, 'naked,' that is, helpless in the grip of decay and death. How indeed could a man so 'crushed' and 'humiliated' and 'dead' to God (Lk 15.24) face his Creator? His wounded sense of his (divine) dignity rose against him. It 'rejected' him, 'abhorred' him, 'repressed' him! So we must accept that his fear at first seems to be organically related to the self-image which the Adamic transgressor saw before him. But on a second examination, verses

12 and 13 lead us to the 'primary' starting point of the fear.

Adam answered God's question about how he came to transgress the commandment and eat of the fruit of the forbidden tree by saying: 'The woman whom you gave to be with me, she gave me the fruit of the tree, and I ate it' (verse 12). This verse is certainly the secret key by which the most fundamental meaning of Adam's frightened behavior towards God can be 'opened' and understood. For by his act of transgression Adam had already also received the (penal) consequences of this act: his physical weakness, decay and death — and of course his separation from God and his hostile relationship with nature. So what is revealed in verses 12 and 13 is the fact that the Adamic couple did not assume responsibility for their act. These two verses transfer the guilt to the woman and to God through the mouth of Adam, and to the serpent through the mouth of Eve. The Adamic transgressor accepted and confessed the act of transgression but he denied his *guilt*. His wounded sense of dignity once again became an object of 'misuse.' Or rather his egoistic impulses, 'hardened' and 'perverted' by sin, 'repressed' his *personal* guilt into the unconscious region of his 'shadow,' into that psychospiritual place of the 'image of God' which had been 'darkened' by corruption. The repression ('denial') of personal guilt was the most substantial consequence of man's psychic conflict, which, after the fall, became solidified as a fundamental process in the psychic life. The inner conflict is identified with what we characterize as the psychic life, and the *repression of guilt* proves to be the most basic function in this life. This shows that the 'primary' starting-point of fear (in the state after the fall) was the direct experience of guilt.

We have already characterized as the 'Adam complex'[9] Adam's behavior from the moment when he was faced with God's commandment to the moment when he confessed the act but denied responsibility and guilt. The correlation between the pattern of Adam's basic conflict and all the psychological theories which attempt to interpret the mental disorder called 'neurosis' leads us to the conclusion that neurosis, as it is described, analyzed and presented by these theories, coincides with Adam's conflict in its basic structure. In both cases the pattern of the basic structure is as follows:

1) The demand of the axiological factor for a certain 'form' ('image') of life.

2) The failure of the biomatic ('individual') factor to actualize this image.

3) The primary genesis of feelings of guilt at having failed to actualize the 'existential outlook.'

4) Repression of the guilty conscience which engenders and maintains the feelings of guilt.

5) Projection of the repression of guilt upon interpersonal relations (in the social field).

6) Neurotic symptoms (mental disharmony, sickness).

Clearly this outline reveals the deepest problem which man experiences as the inner conflict develops. The operation of a guilty conscience in the depth of the human personality is the problem underlined in the biblical text as well. Adam did not seek God's 'forgiveness.' He did not confess his guilt. On the contrary, he pushed the guilt into the dark depth of his 'individuality' corrupted by sin, and with this 'dowry' he was 'sent out of the garden of Eden.' In order that the psychic conflict should not remain and 'live for ever' as a condition basically motivated by a repressed guilty conscience, God 'cast out Adam and caused him to dwell over against the Garden of Delight' (Gen 3.25 Sept.).

As we know, man's return to paradise is realized only through the redemptive power which flows from the cross of Christ. The secret of the healing of man's basic conflict and the cleansing of his guilt lies in the mystery of the redemption in Christ. Man's sanctified conscience 'purified of dark works' becomes the key by which the gate of paradise is opened once more. This possibility for man to recover and sanctify his conscience as a solution to his inner contained in the words of the Prodigal Son: 'Father, I have sinned against heaven and in your sight, and am no longer worthy to be called your son' (Luk 15.21).

PERSONAL AND EXISTENTIAL GUILT (*EXISTENZSCHULD*)

Adam's repression of his personal guilt and the projection of this guilt onto the person of the woman and upon God underlines the deepest and gravest problem of the human personality. In the biblical text man's attitude towards his guilt forms the conclusion to the whole drama of his fall into sin. The transgressor of God's commandment kept his guilty conscience repressed in the depth of his corrupted psyche. He refused to accept this guilty conscience and, as we have said, by this repression he turned it into the basic psychodynamic motive of his behavior.

But what should be noted particularly here is that the whole picture of the fall of Adamic man, and especially his final reaction to God's attempt to make him aware of the repression of his conscience, shows that (sinful) man lives his guilt in two perspectives or spheres. One is the *narrow* sphere of personal guilt in the sense of the concrete act which expresses the violation of God's will. The other is the *wide* sphere of failing to actualize his existential prospect (the 'likeness'). In both cases man feels guilty. In the first he is usually directly aware of his guilt and also reacts to it directly, either through 'forgiveness' or through repression. In the second case he is less aware of his failure to actualize his existential prospect and yet the *guilt* at this failure penetrates his whole existence and lies behind all his psychodynamic functions and reactions.

The Adamic man was not ignorant of his personal guilt, but he denied it, only confessing the act which caused the guilt. Nor was he unaware of the failure of his existential prospect. Perhaps indeed his whole psyche was reacting chiefly to this failure when he tried to conceal his personal guilt. Therefore he was led to a wrong estimation of his entire situation (because of the corrosion to which he had been subjected through sin). He preferred to be expelled from paradise through a denial of his guilt, which (as he thought) would preserve his human dignity, rather than be humiliated and confess the failure of the *supreme* aim of his life.[10] Thus the repression of *personal* guilt serves the purpose of preserving man's existential prospect as far as possible. At the same time, however, this means a life of *existential guilt (Existenzschuld)*.[11]

The primordial picture of the Adamic drama, then, gives us the outline of man's reaction to the most fundamental problem in his existence, the problem of *guilt*. Man is in conflict and torment between his *personal* and *existential* guilts. The *personal* is organically interwoven with the *existential* guilt in such a way that his whole life is a 'complex' dialogue between personal and existential guilt. Man represses and denies his personal guilt in order to protect his existential dignity. And on the contrary, his (unconscious) effort to keep this dignity intact leads him to his *automatic* reaction against acts, weaknesses, shortcomings, neglects and other negative elements in his behavior which create guilty situations in everyday life. We usually repress or do not accept even our smallest weaknesses, or shortcomings and we do not recognize our smallest mistakes, because these micro-guilts unconsciously wound our existential prospect and therefore automatically change the micro-guilt to existential guilt. What would it really cost man if he recognized his micro guilt each time? Certainly the re-establishment (moral and material) of a micro-guilt in the framework of its 'individual' and 'personal' nature is a detail without any special significance in man's personal life. But in its organic relationship with the *existential* outlook this micro-guilt is experienced precisely as *existential guilt*. The drastic corrosion by sin of a man's egoistic impulses (which were supposed to serve constructively towards his becoming 'God by grace') linked his personal and existential guilt together so closely and organically that the 'Adam complex' as a psychic conflict has proved to be the basic process and function in life. Man is usually characterized as an 'egoist' or 'self-centred' or an 'individualist.' In all these, and so many other cases of man's characterization as egoistic, what is alluded to is simply the basic functioning of life: man's use of a psychic conflict to try to assure others and himself that 'as he is, so he *should* be,' or 'he is as he *should* be.' Man cannot tolerate any guilt, either personal or existential. This is why every challenge to become aware of his existential guilt is unacceptable to the same degree as his personal guilt (even a micro-guilt).

The 'Adamic complex,' then, is a (usually unconscious) reaction against any feeling of guilt. Since (or insofar as) man's existential prospect remains unfulfilled, his unconscious psychic system is filled with repressed feelings of guilt. But these repressed guilt feelings intensify his guilty reaction in evey instance of personal guilt as well. So man's basic conflict is a conflict with his existential prospect (the ideal image of himself, the 'likeness'). His guilty conscience is in conflict with this prospect, trying to maintain the 'sense of dignity,' the integrity of a fictitious image of himself.

THE STRUCTURE OF THE PSYCHIC CONFLICT
IN ITS NEUROTIC PICTURE

The term *neurosis* means, in brief, the whole structural system of the basic conflict which is in every person. But the term is used especially in cases where a sharpening of the conflict has magnified the symptoms which reveal the conflict. The 'Adam complex' is the very structure of the basic psychological conflict, setting off the analogous reactions and producing the inexhaustible variety of symptoms by which the always analogous psychodynamic tension of this complex is being studied as the 'neurotic phenomenon' is the sum total of the functional reactions of the 'Adam complex.' We note once again that an unprejudiced study comparing the 'neurotic phenomenon' with the basic picture of Adamic man's psychic conflict and general reactions inevitably results in finding these two processes in man's psychic life to be identical. The 'neurotic phenomenon' is the 'Adam complex' in its concrete, existential form.

This fact permits us to make an organic synthesis of the particular findings of the major depth psychological theories, for their constructive use in examining the human personality in the light of the 'Adam complex.'

In line with this general pastoral psychological approach, we can sketch the essential structure of the neurotic conflict as follows.

a) Every man's basic existential prospect is the 'likeness.' This existential ideal is woven into man's whole psychodynamic being. As we have said, man was made by his Creator with this basic condition and dimension to his existence. He is created and exists in order to be 'in the likeness.' The Christian formulation of the same ideal does not specify its content but simply alludes to it. 'Therefore you shall be perfect, just as your Father in heaven is perfect' (Mt 5.48). Every person, whether or not he has become aware of this ideal, reacts to life's stimuli and its endless variety of challenges under the weight of this fundamental aim of his life: 'to be perfect as his Father in heaven is perfect!'

b) The effective functioning of the 'Adam complex' as a psychodynamic 'heritage' interferes with man's attempt to make an existential *choice* and 'subjects' him to the pressure of 'demonic' suggestion. By 'heredity' ('the sin of the forefathers') man is inclined to prefer the *easier* of the two ways 'to deification.' The 'likeness' requires struggle, toil, self-denial. The demonic suggestion offers an 'immediate taste' of deification in an experience that is always direct, without the struggle and hard effort of the way to the 'likeness.' The 'easy,' the 'beautiful,' the 'convenient' ('good for food . . . *pleasant* to the eyes . . . *beautiful* to contemplate') are the immediate experiences which he seeks and which, according to sin's deception, can quench the insatiable human thirst for deification. Thus man makes the short-term choice, not the long-term one. He now chooses the road offered by demonic suggestion and so refuses the labour or pains of a long-term realization of the 'likeness.'

c) The choice, as a *negation* or *rejection* of the 'likeness' or even as an experience of inability to realize it, means that man is *repressing* this existential ideal. When man chooses one of the two possible ways of being, the other is obviously overlooked and 'scorned.' But this, especially in the case of choosing the demonic suggestion, means *suppression* and *coercion* from within, the 'stifling' of the existential demands of the 'likeness.'

The *repression* of the 'likeness' is really the generative cause of an endless variety of human reactions which contemporary psychology characterizes as *neurotic* symptoms. From Freud to Fromm and Horney, the course of *scientific* developments in psychological research and psychotherapeutic experience is largely determined by the dimensions of the phenomenon of repression. Particularly when Erich Fromm, a synthesist in his existential views, in his work of considerable size and depth, emphasizes the individual's self-repression, he is doubtless presenting an up-to-date summary of the collected conclusions of depth psychology on the most fundamental psychodynamic function in the human personality. The greatest 'accusation' made against man by this psychology is that he represses his genuine, authentic self and *exists* and *reacts* according to the psychodynamic motives of his fictitious self. Both Adler and Horney, more clearly than the other leading depth psychologists, emphasize the 'fictitious' character of the 'ideals' which man attempts to realize when he has repressed his genuine, authentic self.

d) Man's repression of his authentic existential outlook is at the same time a primary source of guilt in him. If one *must* be something, if it is in man's nature to become like the highest being, God, then the only means of satisfying his sense of his own dignity absolutely is to become what he *must* become. Otherwise, the failure to fulfil this goal gives rise to 'guilt anxiety,' the anguish of guilt. This anguish proves to be the psychodynamic motive which leads to *compensation,* to the substitution of a fictitious ideal for the basic ideal. The fictitious image which a person who has repressed the authentic ideal of his life has before him is engendered and activated by guilt anxiety. This explains his uncontrollable passion for various forms or details in life. Although the factors which create man's concrete ('neurotic') reactions are clearly seen in his *superficial* relations to other people and to the conditions and general circumstances of life, the motive underlying all this can only be sought in his basic conflict with his authentic existential outlook. The ultimate basis of this primary conflict in man is always guilt anxiety. But this means a ceaseless (Sisyphean) struggle on man's part to rid himself of guilt anxiety and so to *justify* himself! Every fictitious image of life to which the individual clings passionately and absolutely is directed towards his deepest (and sole) need to neutralize his ('unconscious') guilt feelings, to justify himself. This is why man's strong egoistic reactions and arrogant ('demonic') behavior are the psychodynamic motives in his personality which work with the immediacy of a reflex, of an alarm bell. The egoistic reactions work *automatically* because he feels that he is threatened by on other danger than his *guilt.*

NEUROTIC COMPENSATION AS A CONSEQUENCE OF GUILT ANXIETY

The final *biomatic* expression of the structure of the basic psychic conflict is 'neurotic compensation,' that is the *fictitious* existential outlook adopted by the individual to replace the authentic existential outlook (the 'likeness'). This compensation is characterized as neurotic precisely because it is a product of *repression.* The repression of the authentic existential prospective gives rise to guilt anxiety which exerts a 'compulsive' pressure to *compensate* for this prospect and find release in living in terms of this compensation. Therefore guilt anxiety must be recognized as the starting-point for the endless variety of 'neurotic' symptoms in the individual who is caught up in the 'Adam complex.' Actually, however, the attentive observer of *any* behavior of this individual will notice and appreciate that the individual's efforts at self-justification and projection, at *successes* and *conquests,* are attempts to silence his guilt anxiety, which, though unconscious, is general in its extent, intensity and activity throughout his being.

The basic picture of neurotic compensation for the repressed genuine existential outlook can be seen either in a person's basic model of life or in a combination of many incidental reactions or expressions. In the first case we notice a characteristic exaggeration or morbidity in the individual's behavior. In the second case a careful synthesis of details from the individual's total behavior can show us his fictitious existential outlook. It is not always easy to investigate the structure of a psychic conflict. The symptoms[12] certainly provide a door to the labyrinthian passage of the vicious circle of the conflict. But we must keep firm hold of 'Ariadne's thread of guilt' in order to succeed in reaching the initial source of the conflict and return to the symptom by the same route, to make sure of the organic relationship between the symptom and the psychic conflict which produced the guilt. The labyrinthian character of the investigation which aims, by means of the material of the neurotic symptoms, to put together the whole picture of the compensation is due to the fact that 'the soul is very deep' (St Makarios) and therefore the working or construction of the neurotic compensation passes through the many biomatic layers and other complexities within the psyche. If one remembers that man is tormented not by one complex alone but by a complex of complexes, one can easily understand that the picture of the neurotic compensation cannot be put together on the basis of one symptom or two or three characteristic behavior reactions of the neurotic individual. An understanding of the (neurotic) individual in all the dimensions of his being is required in order to put together the final picture of the neurotic compensation. But as long as guilt anxiety is accepted as the original starting-point of neurotic compensation, the investigator has a

basic guide to lead him from the symptom to the fundamental structure of the inner conflict.

But while this thesis that neurotic compensation is created under
the pressure of guilt anxiety is confirmed by many psychological
investigators and psychoanalysts, their assessment of it is made
at the expense of the human personality. Guilt anxiety is regarded
simply as a psychological defect in the personality, having no essential foundation. According to the conception of most psycho-
therapists and psychoanalysts, 'neurotic anxiety' is *groundless.* It
exists only in the patient's imagination, for, according to 'psychoanalytic logic,' man is never guilty of anything. What he feels as
guilt is a psychological deficiency due, according to the same logic,
to the individual's (unjustifiable) repressions. That is, by interiorizing external prohibitions, the individual tyrannizes himself, treating
himself with the austerity of an external authority. Fromm too has
the same view:[13] 'Man thus becomes not only the obedient slave
but also the strict taskmaster who treats himself as his own slave.'
In this process feelings of guilt arise which unjustifiably tyrannize
the individual. The psychotherapeutic aim of psychoanalysis is to
'rationalize' these feelings and explain them psychologically in such
a way that the individual is 'redeemed' from the morbidity of this
nonexistent guilt. It is just here that psychoanalysis makes its
gravest mistake, in wanting to be redemptive only by making the
patient aware[14] of the unconscious source of his feelings of guilt.
It tries to persuade the neurotic that the guilt feelings which torment him are simply psychological defects due to the repression
of instincts and desires. Or it passes over the guilt problem in order
to proceed to the 'elucidation' of the functioning of the insticts
and drives which, according to its view, are the generative cause
of neurotic compensation.[15]

Thus in the 'discussion' of guilt anxiety psychoanalysis ceases
to be an application of psychological knowledge and becomes an
ideology or an 'existential outlook.' It goes beyond the bounds
of its scientific therapeutic activity and approaches the area of
human existence which is directly determined by its concrete relationship with the *values* of life.

The different approach of psychoanalysis to guilt anxiety shows,
finally, that the picture of neurotic compensation depends not only

on the psychological conditions of the person's life but also on his general appreciation of the values of life. Therefore pastoral psychology, in putting this picture together, refers back to the person's *ultimate* relationship with the highest values in life. Within this framework of the existential dimensions of the personality, neurotic compensation is understood as man's attempt to react to the *commandment* of the 'likeness.'

Although we have already referred to two relevant examples, in the one to follow, taken from Daco,[16] we shall undertake to piece together the neurotic picture as pastoral psychology sees it.

As an example of a 'terrible form of jealousy' Daco refers to one case which is 'moreover, frequent enough.'

Mr. X visits Daco and tells him of the mental torments which he is suffering because of his wife's jealousy. 'My wife constantly accuses me of being the lover of many women whom she knows. She alleges that I make shameful advances to her friends and to all the women I meet. This never ceases. But sometimes it is horrible: really a life of hell. As soon as I get home the ragings and accusations begin, and they follow one after the other without stopping . . . She goes over all my faults. When we are with company it is terrible. Sometimes she goes so far as to make a scene in public and slap a woman in the face whom I have simply looked at in an ordinary way!

'She says that I have many immoral relations with other women and am terribly dissolute . . . Believe me, I am suffering a real martyrdom . . . And what beats all is that my wife knows very well that my so-called mistresses are not at all "my type." '

It is obvious that the psychoanalyst cannot deal with the problem of this tormented husband in a positive way without first having 'analyzed' the wife who displays this destructive jealousy. Therefore it is only after such an analysis that the psychoanalyst reaches his conclusions.

The main conclusion is that the wife is homosexual. But she is 'a latent and unconscious homosexual.' Being an unconscious homosexual, this wife unconsciously desires to make proposals to other women. Why does she not do it? Because her homosexuality is unconscious and because this homosexuality has been repressed from the conscious part of her mind, due to the morality of this wife. Besides, does she not accuse her husband of "sinful" debaucheries and "shameful orgies," which express morally the tendencies that she feels deep down? However the case may be, repressed or not, these unconscious impulses do their work. What is happening then?

1. This wife unconsciously desires to make proposals to women.

2. She cannot and is incapable of doing so.

3. Who, in general, makes proposals to women? Man, that is her husband.

4. At this moment this wife *projects* her own tendencies on her husband. She *becomes* her husband and is convinced that he makes the proposals which she herself desires to make.

5. She is jealous of her husband, in whose position she would like to be in the first place. Then if she is close to her husband there are, moreover, dreadful scenes of jealousy about a mechanism which seems "imaginary" but which is due to strong unconscious tendencies . . .'

And finally Daco sums up the basic conflict in the jealous wife as the opposition between two fundamental motives.

'The wife too is constantly torn by a violent inner conflict between a) her unconscious homosexual tendencies and b) what she thinks she is outwardly: a sexually normal woman.'[17]

This pathological jealousy is dealt with and worked out by the analyst in terms of the Freudian psychoanalytic theory. The analyst sees this woman's psychological resistance to her unconscious homosexual tendencies as forming the structure of her basic conflict. Her jealousy then, according to his view, is a product of this *projection* of the conflict upon the person of her husband who, as a man, has the possibility (and the 'good fortune') not to have such a conflict.

But the jealous reaction which this woman displays towards her husband can also be examined in the light of the conflict between her authentic existential prospect (the 'likeness') and her instictive activity, which leads her to a denial of this prospect. In his description of the case Daco emphasized the activity of the moral factor in the depth of the personality of the jealous wife. He said '. . .this homosexuality has been repressed from the conscious part of her mind, due to the morality of this wife.' And also:

of this wife. Besides, does she not accuse her husband of "sinful" debaucheries and "shameful orgies," which express morally the tendencies that she feels deep down? However the case may be, repressed or not, these unconscious impulses do their work. What is happening then?

1. This wife unconsciously desires to make proposals to women.

2. She cannot and is incapable of doing so.

3. Who, in general, makes proposals to women? Man, that is her husband.

4. At this moment this wife *projects* her own tendencies on her husband. She *becomes* her husband and is convinced that he makes the proposals which she herself desires to make.

5. She is jealous of her husband, in whose position she would like to be in the first place. Then if she is close to her husband there are, moreover, dreadful scenes of jealousy about a mechanism which seems "imaginary" but which is due to strong unconscious tendencies . . .'

And finally Daco sums up the basic conflict in the jealous wife as the opposition between two fundamental motives.

'The wife too is constantly torn by a violent inner conflict between a) her unconscious homosexual tendencies and b) what she thinks she is outwardly: a sexually normal woman.'[17]

This pathological jealousy is dealt with and worked out by the analyst in terms of the Freudian psychoanalytic theory. The analyst sees this woman's psychological resistance to her unconscious homosexual tendencies as forming the structure of her basic conflict. Her jealousy then, according to his view, is a product of this *projection* of the conflict upon the person of her husband who, as a man, has the possibility (and the 'good fortune') not to have such a conflict.

But the jealous reaction which this woman displays towards her husband can also be examined in the light of the conflict between her authentic existential prospect (the 'likeness') and her instictive activity, which leads her to a denial of this prospect. In his description of the case Daco emphasized the activity of the moral factor in the depth of the personality of the jealous wife. He said '. . .this homosexuality has been repressed from the conscious part of her mind, due to the morality of this wife.' And also:

other women in a way absolutely *immoral* or *dissolute*.[18] In this case, however, the jealous wife is not projecting an indefinite aggression on the person of her husband, but a 'guilty aggression.' She is projecting her personal guilt for her own 'bad' and 'morally dissolute' self upon the person of her husband. She feels unconscious guilt about her unconscious homosexual tendencies, which threaten to destroy her 'good idea' of herself. She is struggling then, against her guilt and projecting it unconsciously on her husband in order to get a 'redemptive release.' The 'scapegoat'[19] is the most useful creature in existence. The guilt of others is loaded upon him and he pays the price of their 'conflicts.' Thus the husband in Daco's example becomes the victim of the guilty dialogue which his wife is having with her 'bad' and 'dissolute' self.

In this example, then, as in almost every other case of a neurotic phenomenon recorded in psychotherapeutic and psychoanalytic literature, the outline of a fundamental conflict relating to man's deepest connection with his authentic existential perspective is clearly evident — a connection which gives rise to destructive guilt anxiety. It is to the credit of depth psychology that (despite its exaggerations and errors) it points out all the active *human* psychodynamic motives in the process of the basic psychic conflict. These include, for instance, the moral factor in life and the hidden, unconscious drives as well as the search for a solution to the psychic conflict in the interpersonal and existential areas. On the basis of its own theoretical assumptions pastoral psychology can conveniently make a synthesis of these fundamental elements in every psychic conflict, in order to arrive more easily at the 'human' picture of the conflict. This is why every neurotic phenomenon is recognized as a 'pastoral problem' as well, when one approaches it with the assumptions of pastoral psychology. In any case the basic point at which pastoral psychology concurs with the synthetic picture of the findings of depth psychology is the ultimate basis of the neurotic phenomenon, which, it seems, is always — even in Daco's example — *guilt anxiety*. This anxiety betrays man's conflict with his authentic existential outlook, that is, with himself. Psychology sees man as guilty in his own eyes because he refuses to live by his authentic existential prospect (the 'likeness') and turns to fabrication *false* perspectives. Thus man's psychological problem is also a pastoral psychological problem at the same time, since living with guilt anxiety is the most *universal* human reality. Man cannot repudiate this, even unconsciously!

PART TWO

CHAPTER ONE

THE BIBLICAL MORPHOLOGY OF
THE STRUCTURE OF THE PSYCHIC CONFLICT

THE 'PASTORAL PROBLEM' AS THE PROCESS
OF PSYCHIC CONFLICT

It is the aim of pastoral psychology, as a science belonging to the practical branch of academic theology, to study the nature of the 'pastoral problem.' This problem takes an endless variety of forms. In every case the pastor finds himself confronted with a problem which has a 'personality' of its own.

The concrete factors involved in creating this problem are also different in each case or are related or linked together differently. Yet in spite of this endless morphological variety, pastoral problems can be summed up as one fundamental problem with regard to *structure*. Solving this basic problem leads to the right approach to the particular problems arising from it.

This distinction between the basic and particular pastoral problems derives mainly from viewing each person as a psychosomatic indivisible and coherent whole. A person cannot be regarded as totality of separate problems. To split up the human problem into a number of isolated problems is to lose sight of the *total*[1] existential picture and therefore to be unable to face these problems ᴄontructively from the pastoral point of view.

For this reason every *concrete* pastoral problem must be approached in the light of a basic image of man and thus of the fundamental *structure* of the pastoral problem.

According to this concept, the 'pastoral problem' is a *symptom* of man's *basic* psychic conflict as we have presented it in Part One. But what is the special meaning of the 'pastoral problem' as a *symptom* of the basic psychic conflict?

We should always see the 'symptom' as an *expression* as well as an image of a *concrete* stage in the development of the basic psychic conflict. The symptom is not the psychic conflict itself but, as we have said, a *compensation* (or an attempt at compensation) for a psychic fact which should have been lived under the normal conditions of realizing man's existential prospect.

According to this concept, the symptom is the 'affirmation' of a person's failure to live up to the requirements of his existential prospect (the 'likeness') in an 'orthodox way.' So the *symptom* reveals to us the nature of this failure and, more generally, also the concrete stage of the basic conflict in which the person who has this symptom is living.

As long as we regard every pastoral problem as a symptom of the basic conflict, we must *distinguish* right from the start between the *surface* of the pastoral problem and its *depth*. The surface is the *symptom*. The depth is the basic conflict. This means that every pastoral problem has an outer *form* and an inner structure. Its form is the sum total of the external reactions which constitute the symptom. Its structure is the organic correlation of the factors which work together at the source of basic inner conflict. This is why we are interested in studing a certain morphological variety of pastoral problems in order to see how it is possible to trace our way from the symptom to the depth of the psychic conflict. Indeed since, as we have seen, the *concrete* pastoral problem is a symptom of a certain stage in the development of the psychic conflict, a correct approach to the problem (from the human, pastoral point of view) presupposes that the symptom should be traced back to that stage of the conflict.

Precisely because scientific pastoral psychology is organically dependent upon the soteriological requirements of Orthodox theology and life, the various forms of pastoral problems *indicative* for our study must arise out of Orthodox theology and life. For the present, since we cannot select such problems from all the areas of Orthodox tradition and life, we shall limit ourselves to hagiographic texts. We are obliged by the very nature of *scientific* pastoral psychology to study pastoral problems contained in Holy Scripture (in whatever form). It is by so doing that we can preserve the validity of pastoral psychology as a science in the practical branch of theology, and, moreover, the practical approach to pastoral problems should not be made in the spirit of a purely 'psychological' examination, but above all in the spirit of the revelation 'in Christ Jesus.'

In accordance with this basic thesis, then, we shall select certain texts from the Old and New Testaments which present the pastoral problem in definite forms and at the same time are susceptible of a certain probing.

THE 'PHARISAIC' STRUCTURE OF THE PSYCHIC CONFLICT

Although the *fundamental* structure of the psychic conflict is always the same, that is, it relates to the coordinated functioning of the basic factors in human life, in a *pattern* that is always the same (man's dialogue with his existential prospect), in eveyday life we usually have inexhaustible variations within this basic pattern. The fundamental structure of this conflict is expressed biomatically in many forms and images. One main form is the 'pharisaic' structure of the conflict.

We find this structure in the Lord's presentation of the Pharisee in the parable of Luke 18.9-14. In the first place, the pharisaic structure has two main characteristics: *outward* behavior and *internal* psychodynamic efficiency.

Outward 'pharisaic' behavior. The 'pharisaic' structure of the psychic conflict is *expressed* by the following particular elements.

1) *Excessive* piety of observance of religious formalities. The Pharisee's behavior is dominated by an (anxious) tendency to observe every religious 'formality,' which he considers indispensable for his self-assurance as to his religious superiority. The Pharisee has a *greed*[2] for religious experience.

2) Proclamation of religious perfection. The 'pharisaic' structure of the inner conflict *pushes* this person to proclaim his religious perfection. The Pharisee feels the need to assure, and indeed persuade, other people of his perfection. Therefore he uses *statistics*. The biomatic elements in his piety are *objectified* in such a way as to be measurable and possible to evaluate.

3) *Comparison* of his own religiousness with that of other men. The Pharisee is not communicative in the deeper sense of the word. Yet he needs other men in order to confirm his religious superiority.[3] Although he isolates himself in order to promote his religious superiority, he also invokes other men's weaknesses and shortcomings in order to feel the satisfaction of his religious *self-sufficiency*.

These main characteristics of pharisaic behavior constitute the *mask* which conceals the peculiar structural features of the basic psychic conflict. *Greed* for experience, *objectification* of the biomatic elements of piety, and *dependence* on other people (for comparison) make up the structure of the mask which we characterize as pharisaic. This mask, as behavior, gives the impression of self-sufficiency from every point of view. The Pharisee is the arrogant man ('disdainful' or 'humble only in speech') who has a 'clear' conscience because he is perfect and *faultless* He is, therefore, 'independent' of God and man, because his existential prospect coincides with the self-image which he has created. His mask (his behavior) is identified with this 'idealized' image of himself.

This outward picture of the behavior of the Pharisee shows at first glance that this 'type' faces no existential problems, that he experiences no inner conflicts. Everything in his life goes well. He does not feel that he lacks anything, nor does he have to be envious of anything in the life and behavior of other men.

Nevertheless, just because the external elements of the Pharisee's behavior make up a mask that is perfect in every respect, they are *symptoms* which express and (why not) proclaim the conflict in which he lives. The 'perfect' mask underlines a biomatic inflexibility. This inflexibility is to be understood as an expression of unconscious and indeed compulsive process. Here too, then, symptoms lead us to the place of origin of the Pharisee's psychic conflict.

In fact, the nature of the Pharisee's *perfect* mask (made up of external elements which emphasize the realization of the ideal of religious perfection) shows his problem as well. This problem is the following.

An individual who behaves with moral and spiritual self-sufficiency and has a 'big idea' of himself is essentially deeply disappointed at his inability to be genuinely perfect. His self-sufficiency, therefore, is a result of repressing this disappointment and especially of repressing his guilt at failing to reach his existential goal. The Pharisee struggles for self-justification. He tries in every way to justify himself to himself, to other men, and to God, Yet the fact, as the Lord affirmed, that 'he did not go from the Temple justified' shows that his inner condition was the direct opposite of his appearance of *psychological* self-sufficiency and composure. The effort to show or proclaim his *perfection* reveals the effects of guilt anxiety which, as his chief psychodynamic motive, has led 'inevitably' to the formation of the pharisaic mask.

b) *Inner psychodynamic factors.* Thus the outward pharisaic behavior, composed of particular symptoms, leads us to the *guilty* inner state of the pharisee. The main characteristics of this inner state are the following.

1) *A sense of insecurity.* This feeling is betrayed in the Pharisee's entire behavior and especially in his effort to stress his superiority over other people. Comparison with others is essentially an obsessive dependence on certain supports. Other people are the supports which can prop up his perfection, because usually an individual is more perfect than others in some respect.

But of course the more particular problem which would have to be faced is the question: what is it that the pharisee wants to protect himself from? In other words, what is threatening the Pharisee? It is not difficult to answer this question if we recognize guilt anxiety as the main psychodynamic motive for his behavior. The Pharisee is primarily under the threat of *becoming aware* of his personal guilt at being unable to reach genuine moral and spiritual perfection. If for any reason he became aware of this, the edifice of his fictitious (idealized) self-image would collapse. This would mean a real disaster for him. Thus he tries to make himself secure by comparisons, assuring himself that, since other people are inferior to him, he possesses a perfection which leaves no room for feelings of guilt.[4] Surely, however, the deepest meaning of the Pharisee's insecurity is more closely connected with the fear which he has in facing himself. Primarily he fears his 'naked' (Gen 3.7) self and wants to hide behind the backs of other men in order not to see himself.

2) *A feeling of inferiority.* The psychologically experienced eye is able to recognize any *exaggeration* in human behavior as a *symptom* of a corresponding inadequacy. What is exaggerated in an individual's actions and reactions, then, reveals a largely unconscious process. This is not an arbitrary statement but is based of the fundamental inference in depth psychology which emphasizes the compensating or counterbalancing relationship between the conscious life.

As we have already said, this relationship implies that every repressed psychic 'content' or 'function' has its repercussions in the conscious life, and vice versa. A powerful biomatic experience has its 'complex' links with the unconscious life.[5] Accordingly, the *inflexible* and *perfect* mask of the Pharisee can be understood (mainly in terms of Jung's basic psychological principls) to be a result of strong repressions operating as a counterbalance or compensation. The Pharisee displays an intense feeling of superiority in order to compensate for (or conceal) a strong feeling of inferiority, which is kept pressed down in uncounscious.

Actually if, as we have said, guilt anxiety is the basic psychodynamic motive for the Pharisee's outward efforts to form a mask of superiority and psychological (moral and spiritual) self-sufficiency, then his inner problem is his 'intolerable' feeling of inferiority because of his unrealized authentic existential goal.

3) *Projection of personal guilt upon other people.* The Pharisee's *universal* scorn of other people ('I am not like other men, extortioners, unjust, adulterers' (Lk 18.11) and especially his epitomizing this scorn by pouring it upon a particular individual, reveals his deepest psychic need. Here too the element of exaggeration ('other men') is a symptom of a deep conflict. The Pharisee is in conflict with his guilt, and because he represses it he projects it on the *universal* screen of human nature.[6] All men are worthy of scorn because all men have failed to realize their existential prospect. *All* of them are extortioners, unjust and adulterers. This *generalization* of the guilty state of all men works in the unconscious mind of the Pharisee as a psychological compensation for the need to justify himself. His repressed conscience evokes such an intense guilt anxiety that this generalization is the only psychological relief for him, in his (unconscious) conflict with his unfulfilled existential

prospect (the 'likeness').

But the special 'symptom' of the Pharisee's inner conflict with respect to guilt is doubtless his aggression against others, and the publican in particular. That is to say, the projection of his guilt upon others operates aggresively. The Pharisee is really being aggresive when he compare himself to other men. It is this that makes suspect his self-justification and his attempt to 'prove' his moral superiority. This superiority has no 'personal' self-sufficiency. As we said, he needs 'the backs' of others in order to stand. Therefore he loads them with his personal guilt (by the unconscious mechanism of projection), thereby *destroying* them at the same time.[7] For to load guilt of to any 'scapegoat' also means its destruction. Every 'scapegoat' has to be destroyed.[8]

4) *A feeling of anguish and desperation.* Although anguish is a state rather than a structural element in the psychic conflict as a whole, we must note the *obsessive* character of pharisaic behavior. The Pharisee's anguished attempt to protect himself from any *threat* and his tendency to be aggressive towards every type of scapegoat[9] has already been mentioned. Furthermore, his agression generalized with the feeling of his own absolute self-sufficiency (the Pharisee has no need of God), underlines the anxiety diffused in the Pharisee's behavior. As far as this anxiety springs from the deep guilty substratum supporting the structure of the inner conflict, it also expresses the desperation of the bearer of the pharisaic conflict. This desperation is due to the shattering of the existential prospect in the struggle of everyday life.

The external and internal (psychodynamic) characteristics of the pharisaic reaction readily reveal the structure of the inner conflict which gives rise to these characteristics. This structure is composed of these factors which are organically related to man's attempt to realize his existential prospect *completely.* The basic structure of man's inner conflict is always the same. It varies only as to the particular aspiration of the individual and especially as to the *content* or *type* of compensation for not realizing the authentic existential prospect. The Pharisee aims at 'perfection' after failing to live by his authentic existential prospect. He tries to be 'perfect.' His guilt anxiety fixes his orientation obsessively upon seeking, living and proclaiming perfection. Insofar as this pursuit stems from the repression of his guilt at failing to realize his authentic goal, his perfection is ultimately 'neurotic.'

Thus the distinctive marks of the *structure* of the pharisaic conflict are the *obsessive* quest for perfection, a perfectionist life style and the proclaiming of his perfection — the idealized image. The Pharisee's aim in life is to pursue perfection and to boast that he has acquired it justly and by his own powers.

The pastoral perspective on the pharisaic structure of the psychic conflict. The Pharisee as an object of pastoral care is certainly a 'case,' and perhaps the most difficult of pastoral problems, because the mechanism of resistance in a person who is obsessively impelled towards perfection is very quick to oppose any kind of interference in his personal life. The structure of the psychic conflict of the Pharisee is such that it creates fixed attitudes and hence obdurate reactions to every effort to change these attitudes. As a 'neurotic' person, the Pharisee 'has a very big idea of himself' and therefore considers his presumptuous ideas as genuine ideals. For the same reason he never 'questions their value' but 'rather is proud of them.' This means that to break down his obsessive perfectionism requires a methodical and patient effort of approach to the structure of the inner conflict which maintains the obsession. This approach can be managed only by revealing (unmasking) the 'neurotic perfectionism.' Only when the Pharisee is confronted with the reality of not having succeeded in his existential prospect, may he awaken to an awareness that he must change. Otherwise the attempt to change his attitude towards himself is doomed to failure, since he is so highly primed for 'resistance' and 'self-justification.'

THE 'WHITE GUILT' COMPLEX (Mt 25. 14-30)

The parable of the five talents presents a variety of reactions to one and the same event, the assignment to men of different characters the task of making talents productive. All but one of the servants who receive talents to 'exploit' and turn to account react normally, that is, with 'common sense.' They accept the talents and work to put them to the best possible use.

The servant who has received one talent, however, presents a reaction which is not in accord with common sense and is therefore an *exaggeration* which arouses the interest of the reader of the parable. As we know, the servant who received one talent 'went away and dug in the ground and hid his lord's money' (Mt 25. 18). This act surprises the reader because it is the opposite of what was expected by the lord who had entrusted him with the talent to be used and made productive. Therefore questions arise relating to the psychodynamic starting-point. The main question, of course, is: Why does this servant react in this manner to his lord's *offer*?

Here too the answer depends upon the possibility of looking into this servant's basic inner conflict.

Certainly the structure of the conflict is always the same in its main outlines. The only difference here is in the type of 'existential reaction' which is set in motion by the particular manner in which this servant lives his conflicts. This type is crystallized in one main existential direction and hence shapes itself into a certain kind of 'complex reaction.' That is, while the content is always the same, its expression in everyday life becomes concrete and 'freezes' into a certain kind of reaction. Because this is repeated in the same form and thus constitutes a distinctive mark of the individual, it is characterized as a 'complex reaction' or simply as a complex.

What complex, then, moved the servant who received one talent to behave so unreasonably towards his master?

The answer can be sought in a study of the problem of 'flight' which this servant presents. His action in its totality is one of flight. The characteristic content of his act, the burying of the talent in the earth, underlines the strong compulsion to escape, which is also 'co-accentuated' by the motion': 'he went away.' Psychological support for the interpretation of the 'flight' behavior in this case can be sought in the theory of K. Horney, who analyzes the 'detached' individual, the person who *flees* far from men.

According to Horney, a certain category of neurotic individuals are oriented towards 'moving far from people.' Their neurosis compels them to flee far from people. If we combine organically the two basic reactions of this servant, that is, his act of flight and the 'defence' made to his master, we have in condensed form the picture of the detached individual as Horney presents it.

According to K. Horney, the main characteristics of the detached individual are as follows.

a) The detached individual who moves away from people is first of all alienated from himself. Most neurotics, says Horney, 'shrink from their own inner depths.'[10] This fear leads them to 'a numbness to emotional experience, an uncertainty as to what one is, what one loves, hates, desires, hopes, fears, resents, believes and so forth.' This means that 'detached persons can be quite like the zombies of Haitian lore — dead, but revived by witchcraft: they can work and function like persons, but there is no life in them.'[11]

b) This psychological state of the detached person naturally has its consequences in interpersonal relations. The individual's alienation from himself is lived in everyday life as 'an emotional distance between himself and others.' More precisely the detached person has a 'conscious and unconscious determination not to get emotionally involved with others in any way, whether in love, fight, cooperation of competition.'[12]

c) The detached person's moving far from people is aimed at a 'search for complete independence.' He attempts to achieve this by two means: solitude and self-sufficiency. This is why he is incapable of spontaneous *response* to the demands of everyday life and of working with others or *competing* with them in terms of common sense. According to Horney, 'The detached person is certainly not a conforming automaton. His refusal blindly to concur, together with his aloofness from competitive struggle, does give him a certain integrity.[13]

d) The type of reaction of the detached person which has been emphasized so far indicates that his basic need is not for social superiority or distinction but for a self-sufficient way of life within the sphere of his private solitude. Therefore 'abhoring competitive struggle, he does not want to excel realistically through consistent effort.'[14]

In this sketch of the reaction of the detached person we can really see analytically the picture of the servant who received one talent. We can understand the scriptural words 'he went away' in their deeper psychological meaning as 'alienation from himself.' Since he had *fled* from himself (alienated himself) he had *gone* to the arena of human solitude where he could quietly bury the talent which he had received to use and make profitable. There he made the effort of 'digging' a hiding-place in which to store the talent. Up to this point K. Horney's description of the detached person helps us to understand what existential orientation led the servant in the parable to behave just as he did. It is mainly the servant's 'defence,' however, that explains why he was compelled to submit to this orientation.

In its central meaning the servant's defence coincides with Adam's defence before God. 'He also who had received the one talent came forward, saying, "Lord, I knew you to be a hard man, reaping where you have not sown and gathering where you have not scattered seed. And I was afraid, and went and hid your talent in the ground. Look, there you have what is yours" ' (Mt 25.24-25). This reaction reveals the following psychodynamic motivation.

a) *Aggressive tendency.* The servant is aggressive. This aggressiveness is unjustified. His reaction also surprises the reader of the parable who understands the general spirit of it in connection with the other servants' reaction and the lord's behavior.

b) *Progression of guilt.* The defence attributes guilt to the lord of the talents, because he is 'hard' and 'unjust.' He reaps from fields where he has not sown and collects goods where he has no right to take them, according to the servant's defence.

c) *Reactive fear.* The servant 'was afraid' when he received the talent. The offer of the talent disturbed the 'peace' of his solitude and independence. And this disturbance was manifested as reactive fear, as anxiety. According to Horney, the detached individual can 'get on well' with others as long as he is not emotionally involved. But when anyone intrudes upon him he shows anxiety.[15] Why? Because 'detachment is an intrinsic part of the basic conflict, but it is also a protection against it.'[16] This reaction is common to all neurotics, that is, to all who have a severe conflict. The psychodynamic consequences of the conflict are at the same time the individual's means of protection from the conflict itself. And this is so, just because the neurotic person *represses* the whole psychodynamic system of his conflict. Anything which tends to bring the conflict to consciousness therefore arouses a deep anguish, reactive fear, great anxiety. The lord's offer of the talent to the servant threatens to make his conflict conscious, and he consciously fears this; that is why he reacts with the sensitivity of guilt which we find in his words of defense.

This sensitivity to guilt reminds us of Adam's similar reaction in his own defence before God. Like Adam, the servant too, 'being afraid,' projects his feelings of guilt upon the person of his lord. Again this fact is compelling evidence that the ultimate psychodynamic substratum of the servant's inner conflict is guilt anxiety. His entire behavior is propelled by the strong repression of personal guilt. The reaction set in motion by this guilt — in this case the servant's refusal to assume *responsibility* for the management of the talent — is described as the 'white guilt complex.' The term 'white guilt' here indicates the neurotic's tendency to *avoid* any responsibility which entails the *direct* necessity of making a defence. A neurotic person who is psychologically oriented towards 'detachment' (moving far away from people) tends to avoid accepting any responsibility which would lead directly to the 'rendering of an account,' the *obligation* to make a defence. For this obligation threatens to bring to consciousness the repressed guilt[17] which was created by the psychic conflict (or to which the psychic conflict is due) and also *disturbs* the neurotic 'peace' of the individual.

The 'white guilt complex' as a psychodynamic condition, then, does not indicate that the bearer of the complex is without guilt, but that he reacts in such a way as not to allow any *possibility* of falling into a guilty situation by assuming responsibility. This means that 'white guilt' may not be direct, but it is indirect guilt all the same. Of course, whether direct or indirect, guilt is always guilt, for according to the scriptural saying, 'To him who knows to do good and does not do it, to him it is sin' (Jas 4.17). This is why the servant who buried the talent was not justified by his lord but was judged guilty of not having turned his talent to account and make use of it. 'You ought to have deposited my money with the bankers, and at my coming I would have received back my own with interest' (Mt 25.27).

Finally, for a more particular explanation of the concept of the 'white guilt,' complex, it should be noted that in these words of condemnation the lord pointed out the *least* effort which the detached servant could have made in order not to find himself in the 'dock.' He could have put his lord's money in the bank. This act would have freed him from future guilt and at the same time would have required a minimum of effort. Instead of this, the servant took a more difficult path. He 'went and dug in the ground and hid his lord's money.' The neurotic generally reacts in this unprofitable way. He prefers to be his own oppressor and to spend an enormous amount of psychic energy rather than submit to the normal terms of an interpersonal relationship. For instance, if keeping his 'distance' costs him a great outlay of psychic energy, he prefers this to a simple human relationship. Thus the term 'white guilt' can be used more in those cases in which avoidance of responsibility, while seeming to release the person from the obligation of a 'defence' or from the probability of a 'reckoning,' makes him *clearly* guilty by the very fact of *refusing* to assume responsibility. 'White guilt,' then, is recognized as that other side of a 'repressed' guilt which compels the individual to keep on repressing this guilt. Here once again we see the very deep nature of the 'vicious circle' in the structure of man's basic conflict. The individual who has such a conflict almost always takes the most difficult path in confronting his existential problems. The conflict, like an imprisonment of his inner freedom, does not allow him to take up the simple, normal and therefore less difficult solution. 'White guilt' is seemingly the easiest solution. Refusal to assume a responsibility appears at first as avoidance of imprisonment. Nevertheless, the 'white guilt' complex as enacted by the 'detached' (Horney) servant shows that it is a negative psychodynamic reaction, an imprisonment in the individual's attempt to avoid being imprisoned.

THE STRUCTURE OF 'MATERIAL COMPENSATION' FOR THE PSYCHIC CONFLICT (Lk 12.16-21)

Perhaps the most usual form of expression and way of living the basic psychic conflict is the obsessive pursuit of material security. In this case too exaggeration or a system of exaggerations can certainly lead us to understand the pursuit of material security as a particular form of this conflict. For instance, greed, that is, the obsessive tendency to want and try to have more material goods than one really needs in order to be well off, is an exaggeration which guides the observer towards the source of conflict. Greedy people are bearers of a psychic conflict with a special 'content.'

They are not in pursuit of glory or fame, nor do they desire to force themselves on others socially or politically. Their basic orientation is always firmly bound up with the pursuit of material possessions. This means — also in keeping with what we have said so far — that compensation for the basic psychic conflict can be made in many ways. This particular method of 'neurotic' compensation for the inner conflict, that is, of *repressing* the conflict, is found in characteristic form in the parable of the rich fool (Lk 12 16-21).

Despite the fact that in the case of this parable too we have a characteristic frugality of expression and description, the elements in the rich, greedy man's behavior which are given are enough to give us the picture of 'neurotic' compensation for his basic conflict.

We observe, then, that the *exaggeration* in the behavior of the rich fool is composed of the following psychological reactions.

a) *Egocentrism.* The rich fool uses the personal pronoun 'I' six times in the course of his thinking. This egocentricism is at the same time a clear expression of a 'narcissism' which underlines the absoluteness of his individualistic pursuits.

b) *Social detachment.* The greedy man does not seem to have a family. This may mean that because of his exaggerated individualistic pursuits he is not interested in creating a family, or that under this 'oppressive' power of his pursuits he has forgotten his family. At any rate the characteristic absence of a family framework for his life indicates the greedy man's incapacit for normal family ties.

c) *Independence.* The spirit in which the rich man thinks about how he will use, and particularly maintain, his material goods also excludes any possibility of his working with others. Nothing is said in the parable about co-workers or servants. Despite the fact that the work of 'pulling down' the old barns and building new ones implies the use of workmen and technicians, the rich fool feels this work to be his absolutely private affair. He does not want to be dependent on anyone.

d) *Self-sufficiency.* The abundance of goods which creates the problem of 'what shall I do' accentuates the self-sufficiency which makes him independent of any social or other relationship.

e) *Emotional poverty.* The rich man has no human feelings. The oppressive abundance of his material goods does not help to remind him of people who are suffering undeservedly or undergoing material deprivation in general. He wants all that is his own. He provides nothing for others, not even a 'hypocritical' good thought.

In the case of the rich fool too we would say that K. Horney's theory of the 'detached' person who moves away from people applies perfectly. The special characteristics of the detached person which come to the fore in connection with the rich man's material pursuits are as follows.

a) *Resourcefulness.* According to Horney, 'the most positive expression (of the detached person) is resourcefulness . . . He has to be resourceful in order to live. It is the only way he can compensate for his isolation.'[18] The rich fool finds his own solution to his problem, that is, he 'invents' a way to deal with the abundance of his material goods which will give him the full benefit of them.

b) *Independence.* 'Self-sufficiency and privacy both serve his most outstanding need, the need for utter independence.' The detached person 'as a rule prefers to work, sleep, eat alone.' This tendency obviously compels him to be isolated from any connection with family or other relatives. Perhaps this is why family ties are not mentioned in the parable.[19]

c) *'Social indifference.'* According to K. Horney, the detached person 'wants *not* to be involved, *not* to need anybody, *not* to allow others to intrude or to influence him . . . There is a general tendency to suppress all feeling, even to deny its existence . . . The rejection of feeling pertains primarily to feelings towards other people and applies to both love and hate. It is a logical consequence of the need to keep at an emotional distance from others.'[20]

d) *The tendency to do a minimum amount of work in his life.* The detached person 'is inclined to restrict his eating, drinking, and living habits and keeps them on a scale that will not require him to spend too much time or energy in earning the money to pay for them.'[21] The obsessive tendency to isolate himself normally creates in the detached person the conviction that he has a self-sufficiency which frees him from having to enter into competitive dialogue with others. He thinks that there is no reason for special and consistent efforts to increase his material goods. 'Productiveness' comes of itself. Therefore 'abhorring competitive struggle, he does not want to excel realistically through consistent effort. He feels rather that the treasure within him should be recognized without any effort on his part . . . In dreams, for instance, he may picture stores of treasure hidden away in some remote village.'[22]

e) *Obsessive 'security.'* According to Horney, 'the neurotic trends involved in detachment give the individual a feeling of security as long as they function, and . . . conversely, anxiety is aroused when they fail to function. As long as the detached person can keep at a distance he feels comparatively safe.'[23]

The parable of the rich fool can be seen as a summary of these characteristics, for the main points in the rich fool's reaction are the same as those of the detached (neurotic) person. This correlation helps us to understand that pathological attachment to material goods, precisely as it is presented in the parable, is more expressive of a deep psychic conflict than simply of a normal mental state. This conflict is revealed by the *foolishness* of the rich man. The foolishness lies in the fact that he transforms a simple human tendency (the enjoyment of material goods) into the primary (and indeed sole) aim and rule of life. This means that he absolutizes a relative value in life — material goods (Caruso). This absolutizing is really the rich man's compensation for the failure of the basic aim of his life. His failure to be perfected in the spirit of the demands of the 'likeness' leads him (through his inner conflict) to choose a basic goal which has an absolute character. The rich man's 'pathological' attachment to material goods then is a substitute for trying to be perfected according to his authentic existential outlook.

We can examine the way in which compensation for the aim in life works from another point of view, that of the 'transference.' 'Transference' is an unconscious psychic phenomenon associated with strong repressions. It is a special kind of 'projection' and is usually observed in interpersonal relations.[24] For instance, a neurotic person undergoing analysis may transfer to the analyst his conflict with his father. But such a 'transference' of a conflict can take place in other existential settings as well. In the case of the rich fool we have an *internal* transference. This man *transfers* an existential *moral* problem from the realm of conscience to the realm of material survival. This transference is due precisely to the severe repression of feelings of guilt, an existential guilt which arose out of his failure to realize the authentic existential prospect. This explains his 'passion' for material goods, which takes a universal position in his life. The rich fool is attached to material goods 'unto death.'[25] The obsessive character of this attachment is uncontrolled and unmanageable. The rich man can neither control this attachment nor make use of it in connection with his other inner tendencies and inclinations. This helplessness also determines the existential consequence of his 'passion': his ruin. Without inner freedom he is inevitably brought to a general disaster. The divine reminder: 'You fool! This night your soul will be required of you; then whose will those things be which you have provided?' (Lk 12.20) reveals the *vanity* of the fictitious existential outlook of the rich fool. His 'pathological' attachment to material goods was not a fulfillment of his authentic existential goal but a 'wreaking' of its utter destruction.

So the structure of the 'material' compensation arising from the rich man's basic inner conflict is identical to that of an unconscious 'transference' of the problem of the repression of existential guilt. This problem is transferred, through repression, from the field of moral awareness to the framework of pathological attachment to material goods.

Consequently the *pastoral prospect* for confronting greed must be oriented towards uncovering the problem which this 'passion' conceals. The spirit of the divine reminder is aimed at revealing the existential vanity of the greedy man. This man must be convinced of his moral and spiritual inadequacy and consequently of the futility of his existential goals. The pastoral dialogue must aim to evoke sobriety and vigilance, in the spirit of the divine reminder. Since the attachment to material goods is taken as safeguarding existence, the greedy person must be 'transferred' by the pastoral dialogue to a state of *sober insecurity*. The challenge: 'then whose will those things be which you have provided' must dictate the spirit of this dialogue so that the greedy man's basic position will be shaken continually. When he understands that material goods do not safeguard the deeper foundation of his existence, he can cooperate in a reexamination of his 'fictitious' existential outlook.

THE 'JUDAS COMPLEX'

In the *religious* life too the basic conflict takes an endless variety of forms. A religious individual may certainly live the gospel truths strugglingly but consistently to the best of his ability. Yet not even this individual can be considered completely free of conflicts that disturb his progress towards spiritual perfection. One symptom of inner conflict found mainly in religious people is the appearance of the 'Judas complex' as a way of reacting to the incriminating challenges of the environment.

But what we mean in particular, by the 'Judas complex'?

a) In the first place we mean the religious individual's *aggression* towards the guilty image of Judas. As a rule most Christians have the worst idea of Judas. It has been rightly observed that 'in the Christian mind the figure of Judas has always been very repugnant and he has been regarded as preeminently the instrument of Satan,'[26] and likewise that 'the Christian world has been accustomed to seeing Judas as the embodiment of man's inner opposition to God.'[27] Judas is *par excellence* the guilty person in the circle of those who surrounded the Lord in his human life. He is the one who betrayed the Lord. So it is natural that he brings upon himself the anger and 'hatred' of the 'Christians' for his ignominious and treacherous act. The readiness with which a religious person attacks Judas can be characterized as the 'Judas complex.'

b) Any reaction of 'guilty sensitivity' can also be characterized as a 'Judas complex.' For instance, in Judas's case when the Lord said at the Last Supper: 'He who dipped his hand with me in the dish will betray me . . .' Judas, who was betraying him, said: 'Rabbi, is it I?' (Mt 26.23-25). That is to say, whenever a religious person (or in this second case any person) is faced with an incriminating challenge it is possible to react by asking (or wondering): 'Can I be the guilty one?' This reaction is probably in most cases sparked off by Judas complex.

The Judas complex then can be understood in two ways: 1) as an attack against the guilt of Judas, and, 2) as the reaction of a personal sense of guilt.

Although at first sight it seems that we are dealing with two reactions with opposite psychological orientations, in fact one and the same complex is always operating in both cases. The difference is only that the thrust of the complex in the first case is towards an offensive against guilt, while in the second case it is towards 'submissiveness' to guilt. The primary cause of both of these reactions to guilt lies in the 'symbolic' attitude which (mainly) religious people have towards the guilty 'archetypal' image of Judas.

Because of the important role which Judas played in that significant event in the human life of the Lord, his 'arrest' by his
crucifiers, Judas has indeed been invested with the psychological
authority of an archetypal image in the unconscious.[28] The 'collective' religious unconscious of every Christian contains the 'archetype of guilt,' Judas. When this archetype is called forth by
similar guilty connections which a religious person has with other
people, it impels him to react correspondingly. The operation of
the Judas complex is easiest to understand in the aggressive reaction of the religious individual against the 'image of Judas.'

Indeed religious people, as folkloristic material also shows,
sometimes bring their aggressions against Judas to a climax by
burning his effigy. Psychological study of this aggressive reaction
can easily show that such action has absolutely no 'objective' meaning. Since any aggression raises a suspicion of an unconscious reaction, such a drastic act as the burning of an effigy of Judas, often
in frenzied celebrations, clearly points to an unconscious relaxing
of inner tension. The burning of Judas can be understood better
psychologically as a variant of the 'scapegoat' complex. Judas's
act provides religious people with an easing of their guilty repressions and thus for getting relief (unconsciously) from guilt which
torments them without their realizing it.

A *positive* attitude shown by a religious (?) individual towards
Judas' betrayal is, however, particularly characteristic of the Judas
complex. As we know, certain individuals are dominated by the
idea that Judas's act was absolutely indispensable in order for
Christ's sacrifice to be accomplished. Without the betrayal, they
maintain, it would not have been possible for Christ to reach the
martyrdom of the Cross.[29] It had been foretold by prophets.
Therefore Judas was an instrument of divine providence,
cooperating in the work of the salvation of man by Jesus Christ.

C. G. Jung's analysis of a story relating to this attitude gives
us an opportunity to observe the functioning of the Judas complex
in its most expressive form. In his effort to analyze the *symbolic*
meaning of the betrayal of the hero in general, Jung compares an
example from the work of Anatole France: *The Garden of Epicurus*,
which contains the extraordinary story of the Abbé Oegger.[30]

This priest, as presented by the writer, was worried by the thought of what the final fate of Judas was. The problem with which he was vitally concerned was whether Judas was really condemned to everlasting punishment, as the Church teaches, or whether the loving God forgave Judas and justified him, since he was used as an instrument to the work of man's salvation through Jesus Christ.

The Abbé Oegger showed that he preferred to accept the second version. He preferred to accept that God 'in his supreme wisdom' had chosen Judas as an instrument foreordained to act in the most critical hour of Christ's redemptive work. Since Judas's mission was so necessary and so important, he could not possibly be condemned by God. But since Oegger wanted to be convinced of Judas's justification, he betook himself one night in the church and implored God to give him a sign that Judas was saved. And in fact, as he declared, while he was praying in the church he felt a heavenly touch on his shoulder. The next day Oegger hurried to his bishop to inform him of his resolve to work as a missionary in order to preach the gospel of God's infinite goodness, mercy and forbearance.

At this point Jung asks why the abbé was worried about the problem of the ultimate fate of Judas. Jung himself hastens to explain it with the information that by going out into the world to preach the gospel Oegger found his opportunity to satisfy an inner desire: to join the Swedenborgian sect. This means that he had long been preparing for a 'betrayal.' This betrayal gave him feelings of guilt. So, wanting to rid himself of these feelings, he tried to ensure God's mercy beforehand. This makes it plain that this priest was 'Judas.' For a long period of time he had been living and reacting as 'Judas.' His behavior towards his bishop was guided by the 'Judas' complex.

So we see in the case of the priest Oegger how the unconscious (repressed) guilt system (or anguish) worked in the depth of his personality. Oegger projected upon the guilty image of Judas his own personal guilt which had been created by his intention to change his 'dogmatic' position. In this projection he *identified* himself psychologically with Judas. This shows us that the search for certainty about the ultimate fate of Judas had not really been that of the Abbé Oegger but that of the *Judas* Abbé Oegger. It was Oegger become *Judas* who entreated God in the church to give him a sign of Judas's redemption.

This story of Oegger is a typical sample of the versatility of the Judas complex, its many possible expressions. It has not only one psychodynamic function but more than one. Yet it can always be understood mainly as an unconscious tendency to justify a personal guilt. The queries 'Am I guilty?' or 'May I become guilty?' or 'Am I *considered* guilty? derive from a deep sense of guilt which of necessity puts the system of self-justification into motion. But the Judas complex often prompts aggression in interpersonal relations as well. Anyone who is in fact a Judas or feels like Judas (because of a real and conscious guilt) projects his guilt on every neighbor who can fit the role of a scapegoat. Thus the other person very easily becomes 'Judas' and hence the object of guilty aggression from the one who is really *Judas*.

Religious people's aggressions against Judas on the one hand and their 'protection' and 'defence' of Judas on the other, then, are derived from the same psychodynamic motive. In both cases the starting-point is a personal problem: a strongly repressed personal guilt. This means that the Judas complex has multiple functions and is sustained psychodynamically by one basic motive, the *repression* of personal guilt.

The pastoral goal in treating the 'Judas' complex should be to help the *dissociate* the religious individual's personal guilt from the guilty image of Judas, especially whenever this complex is manifested with striking directness. The pastoral dialogue should undertake to draw the line of demarcation between the personal guilt of the religious individual and the 'symbolic' guilt of 'Judas' or any other Judas who is being used as a 'scapegoat' by the religious individual.

AGGRESSION AS A GUILT STRUCTURE AND AN EXPRESSION OF PSYCHIC CONFLICT

When we examine the basic psychic conflict in the light of 'existential guilt,' the structural outlines of man's general aggressive behavior become relatively clear. Aggression, a characteristic element in individual and group life, is one of the most habitual reactions. Almost every human being expresses himself *aggressively* to a great extent. This statement can be accepted more easily if one looks at the findings of depth psychology on the subject. According to these findings, man's aggressive behavior is not always expressed through *direct* and *manifest* destructiveness. Man (every person) knows how to be aggressive, in many cases 'with gloves on.' He 'attacks' with a smile and destroys on the holiest of pretexts.

The very fact that man is more aggressive than he appears or than he thinks, gives broader dimensions to the problem of the primary source of human aggression. Certainly from what we have said so far about the structure of the basic conflict, it is evident that this is the source; human aggression springs directly from the seat of the basic conflict. But this view is affirmed by many biblical sources for the sake of emphasizing that man himself, and not the external circumstances of his life, is originally to blame for his aggression. This verification within the biblical field is therefore very significant for man's effort to study the problem of aggression and find out the right way to solve it.

The parable of the unforgiving servant (Mt 18.25-35) then gives us a basic image of guilt in which we can see the starting-point of human aggression. According to this image, aggression is organically linked with an *unfulfilled* obligation. This basic element in the image of guilt in the parable of the unforgiving servant naturally leads us once again to the outline of the structure of the basic conflict as we have sketched it so far. For the servant's *debt,* as understood from its existential consequences,[31] is an existential obligation and not merely a material one. Therefore this debt can be identified with man's *moral* obligation to live up to his authentic existential outlook.

Indeed the spirit of the parable, in combination with the individual images, leads us to a deeper understanding of a person's relationship with himself. If man's aggression begins from within, he must look for the prime factors of his aggression not in his social surroundings, but in the dimensions of his existential orientation. If a man is urged by an inner need to be aggressive, he must concern himself with learning what are the sources of this inner need.

As long as one is led back to man's existential problems in the search for the original source of human aggression, one will understand that in any case this source lies in the area of the 'hostile relationship' between the individual's ego and his repressed existential guilt. For it is self-evident that what the individual *represses* and refuses to admit freely and consciously into his awareness is disliked and condemned by him. This behavior of the ego seems clearest in Jung's theory, which outlines the process of repressing a psychic content or function. The complex in which the age is *identified* with the content or function which it represses gives us a grasp of the full intensity of the 'controversy' between these two basic factors in every psychic conflict. The ego 'hates' what it represses. But what is repressed 'takes revenge' by immediately imprisoning the ego in the region of the unconscious forces. It is in this hostile relation between the ego and the repressed psychic reality that we must look for the original source of human aggression, and not in any external ('social') factor.

In the parable of the unforgiving servant, aggression is vividly presented as a guilt structure and an expression of the psychic conflict, in the *striking* reaction of this servant after his master releases him from his debt. The reader or hearer of the parable expects, as the inevitable 'logical' outcome that the forgiven servant will respond in a similar way to the debt of his fellow servant. The disproportion between the two debts makes it all the more self-evident that the wicked servant will behave kindly towards his debtor. Instead of this, however, he displays an intense and humiliating aggression towards his fellow servant. 'But that servant went out and found one of his fellow servants who owed him a hundred denarii; and he laid hands on him and took him by the throat, saying, "Pay me what you owe!" So his fellow servant fell down at his feet and begged him, saying, "Have patience with me, and I will pay you all." And he would not, but went and threw him into prison till he should pay the debt'(Mt 18.28-30).

The 'absurdity' of this reaction of the wicked servant to his fellow servant surely has a direct connection with unconscious processes. What we cannot understand logically in human behavior prompts us to look for unconscious sources of a psychic reaction. According to this 'psychological logic,' however, the absurdity of the wicked servant's reaction can only lead us to the seat of a severe inner conflict. For this reason we can understand the surprisingly intense aggression towards his fellow servant as hurled against himself, with whom he is in conflict in the first place. That is to say, if the debt of the wicked servant is really *existential,* it is an outward expression of the inner problem. This problem is the intolerable and burning sense of guilt at his failure to measure up to the requirements of the ideal image of himself. The wicked servant is angry with himself because his Lord's tribunal' has found him guilty of an incalculable debt, which he was not in a position to pay and in the end did not pay. The 'release' from the debt does not soften the wicked servant's anger with himself, because the process of this release has contributed to making him aware of the dimensions of his guilt rather than to any sense of being 'justified.' The remission, then, has increased his anger with himself and intensified his sharp feelings of guilt about his incalculable debt. So as soon as the wicked servant finds himself faced with his own debtor, he is prompted to react as if against himself, with the same anger and the same aggression.

As K. Horney observes, 'We shall not understand the neurotic's rage at himself or the dimensions it assumes unless we keep in mind how immeasurably important it is for him to maintain the illusion that he is his idealized image.'[32] This observation coming from clinical experience affirms the reality of the guilt structure in the wicked servant's aggression and confirms that this structure is an expression of the basic inner conflict. This *expression,* which, according to Horney, can take on unpredictable dimensions, is to be understood mainly as a *projection* of this aggression upon other people. With the eyes of his unconscious the wicked servant sees the other servant as his own self. So in taking his fellow servant by the throat, he is taking himself by the throat. His guilt reaction is intended to relieve the inner pressure caused by the burning feelings of guilt. But this reaction is of no avail. For it is expressed only as a 'symptom' of the vicious circle in which anyone is involved who represses his existential guilt. Therefore, in spite of his master's compassion, the wicked servant does not escape disaster after all. The parable ends with the report that the master delivered the wicked servant 'to the torturers until he should pay all that was due to him' (verse 34). Psychologically this could mean that the master delivered the wicked servant to the torturers 'of his inner psychic tribunal' so that in this way he might understand his guilt, accept it, and sincerely and frankly seek forgiveness.

The pastoral perspective on *guilt aggression* should be focused on the wicked servant's arrogant assertion that he would be able to repay the immeasurable debt to his master. 'So the servant fell on his knees, imploring him, "Master, have patience with me, and I will pay you all" ' (v. 26). The neurotic, as Horney said, strives to 'maintain the illusion that he is the idealized image.' So he persists arrogantly in his conviction that he embodies this image very well. This means that every attempt to cast doubt on this embodiment enrages the neurotic and arouses his aggression. The pastoral dialogue should be directed towards clarifying the projections of guilt upon other people. These projections are organically interwoven with all the guilty concatenations of the basic psychic conflict as a whole. The aggressive person must come to understand whom he is hitting when he attacks his neighbor. The pastoral dialogue should expose this aggressiveness as an expression of his basic psychic conflict and therefore as the guilt structure of that conflict.

THE 'ESAU COMPLEX'

The social role played by each person at a given moment is to be understood as a complex psychological function at the same time. This means that the role has many dimensions and it is not always possible to extract a particular one of them without referring directly to the complex nature of its psychological structure.

Nevertheless, the point of departure for a general examination of the role which the individual acts out within the system of his human ('social') relationships must essentially be an inquiry into the way in which this individual is taught to accept or reject his 'social' role (or roles). For as we know, the role is preexistent to the individual. Although it is possible to shape an individual, or specialize the function of a role in accordance with his individual existential 'specifications,' there always exists *a priori* a structure of social roles which is an inalienable 'establishment' in human existence. For instance, the roles of father, mother, priest, teacher, leader, pupil, and others are social functions which exist prior to the individual. Thus as soon as a person is born he enters in some way into the niche of the role imposed on him by the 'established' social structure.

In the first place then the necessity of the role is an objective characteristic of the structure of society in general. But every individual, as we have said, has a right to relate to this objective command of his particular role in a subjective way. Thus, eventually, the specific aspects or functions of social roles are shaped and small or great changes or reforms are brought about in some structures of the individual and collective (social) life.[33]

Research into the individual's way of living a role is a matter for social psychology.[34] That science endeavors to define the laws by which the different roles function and to determine the factors which together work to create those laws. In order to do this it studies the individual's social reactions in small or large groups. One such group, which is always considered to be the basic substructure of social life is the *family*. Within his family life the individual is taught to converse in this or that way with his social roles. The necessity of a role already appears within the sphere of the family. So the individual's social awakening inevitably takes place within the necessity of the social roles which family life imposes on him. He does not comprehend beforehand whether or not social roles exist, and by the time he awakens socially he already feels subjected[35] to the necessity of one or more social roles. What are the probable reactions of an individual who perceives in some way that he is 'trapped' in the niches of a role or roles?

The way in which an individual will live the role which his position in the structure of the family life imposes upon him is naturally always determined by both internal and external factors. Not only the psychological and spiritual conaracteristics of the individual, but also the other factors of family life will have a decisive influence on the way in which the individual reacts to taking up and living his particular social role. At this point the reader should refer not only to the views of psychoanalysis but also to other psychological and educational theories in order to understand the depth and breadth of the research that has been done on the shaping of an individual's attitude to the demands of the particular role which he is to play in the family and the wider social environment. These references provide the framework for looking at the reaction of Esau, son of the patriarch Isaac (Gen 25.31-34), to the necessity of taking up the role of the firstborn child in the family.

As we know, Esau 'despised his birthright' for a 'mess of pottage' (Gen 25.34). The passage about Esau's reaction is one of the best known texts in the Old Testament. There is surely no Christian who is not familiar with this incident in which bodily fatigue and hunger made Esau consent to abdicate his property rights and social role (Gen 27.37) as the first-born child of the family. So such acts are still today often referred to typologically, for instance in the phrase 'He sold his field (or something else) for a mess of pottage.'

But the question which can lead to a deeper explanation of the causes of Esau's renunciation of his birthright and so possibly throw light on this type of reaction against taking up a social role is: How did Esau reach this critical point of scorning his social privileges? For the birthright did not only impose obligations but like every genuine social role, it also assured certain privileges. Indeed the fact that Esau 'lifted up his voice and wept' (Gen 27.38) when he understood the consequences of his renunciation shows that his act was not completely free, and in some way not fully 'conscious.'

Indeed the observant reader of this biblical text notices first of all that there is a great disproportion between the despised social value (of the birthright) and what he received in exchange ('bread and stew of lentils'). Therefore the question also arises: Who was it that led Esau to this unfavourable exchange?

Careful observation of the biblical passages which present aspects of the relations between Esau and Jacob, as well as between him and their parents (Isaac and Rebekah), clarifies the basic picture of the origin and development of the inner conflict which led Esau to despise his birthright. To be sure, the reason which Esau gave was bodily fatigue and exhaustion to the point of death. 'Look, I am about to die; so what profit shall this birthright be to me?' (Gen 25.32). But it is well known today that great bodily fatigue may be a result of mental exhaustion due to severe inner conflicts.[36] Esau's inner conflict may have been directly connected with his position in the family and especially with his relationship to his mother and his brother.

Despite the meagerness of the biblical grounds for affirming that Esau's renunciation of his birthright was caused by an inner conflict, they do provide a foundation on which this affirmation can be established psychologically.

First of all, in verse 27 of Genesis 25 the general character types of the two competing[37] brothers are defined with exceptional clarity. 'Esau was a skilful hunter, a man of the field, but Jacob was a mild man, dwelling in tents.' Esau was a man of the field and the hunt, while Jacob was a 'child of the home.' Thus conditions were naturally created for special emotional and psychological relations between the children and their parents, as the next verse tells us. 'Isaac loved Esau, because he ate of his game; but Rebekah loved Jacob.'

The strength of Rebekah's maternal tie with Jacob is perhaps the principle clue to the chief factors in Esau's inner conflict and to its whole development.[38] As the findings of psychology and education show us, the multiple existential bond with the mother (forming the biological, psychological-emotional and moral condition of the child's life)[39] has a decisive influence on the formation of a person's general response to the stimuli of life. Thus Esau very quickly became aware that his brother was the special object of their mother's love, while he himself met with niggardly affection and sympathy from her. Every time Esau returned tired from his work in the fields he entered an atmosphere which, if it was not hostile to him, was not very 'intimate' at any rate.

This situation, which Esau faced every time he went home, was created mainly by two extremely destructive factors: maternal emotional privation on the one hand and, because of this, the competitive superiority of his brother on the other hand. His mother and his brother strangled him psychologically and made him more and more aware of his inferior[40] position in the family. Furthermore, according to the findings of depth psychology, it must be seen as self-evident that Esau would tend to repress this awareness of his inferiority. For as he realized that as the firstborn child he had a certain role to play in the family and society, it was reasonable not to want to acknowledge a social defeat.[41] So in the end he was in conflict not only with his mother and his brother but also with *himself*.

Thus he foresaw that with the passage of time, as he neared the age of taking up his role, his 'opponents' would get stronger and the danger of a humiliating loss of his birthright through their superiority would become more and more immediate. Moreover, the next event already demonstrated that Esau's fear was justified when, at the instigation of their mother and with her help, Jacob cheated him out of his father's blessing (Gen 27.1-40). So Esau, caught in the vicious circle of his inner conflict, decided (consciously or unconsciously) to give up the demands of his role. By some pretext or pretence he could, as he thought, withdraw with greater dignity. Therefore he looked for an opportunity to abandon the privileges of his role.

Perhaps we may surmise that this opportunity had been prepared with great care by Jacob himself, always with his mother's help. Physically (and psychically) tired, Esau came home one day to the sight of some very tempting food. So he made a strong request for a little food. 'And Esau said to Jacob, "Please feed me with some of that same red stew, for I am weary" ' (Gen 25.30). It was a very critical moment for Jacob, who wanted to get possession of the birthright. So he asked for the birthright in exchange. He understood that Esau was 'ripe' to capitulate without other conditions. And Jacob did not fail, for Esau had been waiting for such an opportunity. With the emphasis which he placed on his bodily (and mental) fatigue he showed that he was really ready to 'fail.' His answer: 'Look, I am about to die; so what profit shall this birthright be to me?' was an exaggeration which can be seen only as an expression of his deep inner conflict within the family scene. Under no other circumstances would a firstborn son give up his birthright for a plate of stew. Perhaps Esau, confronted with his brother's offer, thought: 'I am so tired of my humiliating position in this house that I sometimes think that death is the only solution to my problem. So what have I to gain by making a struggle to the death to keep the privileges for which the others consider me unfit? I 'll take this chance to give them up and so escape from the net of my inner conflict.' In the end, however, Esau was not released from this net but was overpowered by it.

We have already presented the net[42] which can be characterized as the 'Esau complex.' This phrase can always be used to defined the psychological state of one who is looking for an escape into defeat or resignation from the responsibilities of a social role or duty.[43]. A person who for any reason has strong feelings of inferiority and wants to be freed from the inner conflict created by his constant defence against these feelings is always on the point of wanting to resign and abandon the struggle to keep this defence. Likewise anyone who is mentally tired of his struggle to live up to a social role and who abandons this role on a cheap pretext ('for a mess of pottage')[44] is behaving just as Esau did. He has an 'Esau complex.' He thus rejects — not directly, but indirectly — a role which has been thrust upon him by the social structure within which he lives and moves. This rejection, as he thinks, frees him from the sharp feelings of guilt (which are generated by the sense of his social inadequacy) and preserves the 'integrity' of his idealized image (Horney). But of course the reality is not quite as he 'thinks.' His reaction does not free him but puts him still more firmly in the grip of the basic structure of his conflict. For this reason his reaction is that of a 'complex.'

CHAPTER TWO

THE BIBLICAL MORPHOLOGY OF
THE SOLUTION TO THE PSYCHIC CONFLICT

THE QUESTION OF SOLVING THE PSYCHIC CONFLICT

The growing awareness of inner conflict is a fact noticed by every observer of human behavior. Everyone concerned with the study and treatment of human problems can easily see that man is in conflict with himself. Certainly the psychologists investigating the depths of the human personality have largely grasped the way in which the psychic conflict operates in general. As we have seen, studies of this operation lead to various problems of disagreement among researchers as to their basic views of it. The broad problem areas connected with the psychic conflict relate to its *aetiology, structure, symptomatology* and *effects* upon individual and group life. But these problems all together refer to only one general aspect, the study of how the inner conflict functions. The other general aspect which attracts the greatest interest of research refers to the question of solving the psychic conflict. How can the inner conflict be resolved in a way that is really redemptive for the sufferer?

It is obvious that in each the answer given is organically related to the theory by which the *aetiology* and *structure* of the conflict are interpreted. That is, the deontology of the solution to the conflict necessarily depends on the particular theory of its origin and structure. Thus we come to the most critical problems of this conflict. For if man's fundamental existential problem is (and should be) a single one, then only one solution should be authentic. But if the aetiology of the conflict is determined in each case along the lines of a particular theory about this basic existential reality

of human life, then there must be as many 'sound' solutions offered as there are theories which aspire to study and answer the
ultimate question of the *way* to resolve the conflict. Therefore the
question of a solution to the psychic conflict is the most sensitive
problem facing pastoral psychology. In the area of this problem
the existential depth or breath of the basic conflict, which is
ultimately identified with man's whole existence, can be understod
more clrearly.

At this point clarification is needed with regard to the *structure* and particular functional aspects of the psychic conflict. As
we saw in the preceding chapter, the basic structure of the conflict should be investigated in the light of the morphological variety
which the biblical texts contain. The general conclusion drawn from
the investigation is that this structure is a result of man's conflict
with his existential outlook. The existential guilt resulting from
his failure to actualize the 'likeness' is the motivation power of
the entire 'mechanism' of this conflict. Hence the solution of the
psychic conflict as presented in the biblical texts should be
organically connected with a direct confrontation of this guilt in
accordance with the terms of Orthodox soteriology. Therefore just
as we have sought the structure of the psychic conflict within the
patterns of human behavior and reaction contained in these texts,
so too we shall seek the method and morphology of its solution
in the biblical texts. The emphasis on *one* authentic solution
doubtless seems to contradict this morphology, that is, the variety
of *methods* of solving the conflict. But this is only a seeming con-
tradiction. For while there is usually a single solution to a problem, the methods by which the solution can be reached may be
(and usually are) more than one. If, then, the relationship between
the interpretation of the *aetiology* of the basic psychic conflict and
the deontology of its solution is organic, there is surely only one
solution. But the methods by which this solution can be brought
about are many, for they depend upon the concrete conditions of
the personal life of he bearer of the conflict. For this reason we
can speak of a biblical morphology of the solution to the psychic
conflict. The one solution has many methods ('forms').

The morphology (the variety of ways) of solving the inner conflict can also be understood from the purely psychological point

of view, and this is justifiable. For, as we have said, spiritual experiences have a psychological backbone, a psychological basis.[1] There always exists a *biomatic* distinction between a psychological and a spiritual fact or phenomenon. This means that the evolving solution to the psychic conflict necessarily follows *definite* psychological grooves and psychodynamic channels. Psychological research (despite the variety of theoretical views) has arrived at basic verifications accepted by psychological 'common sense.' As we have said, repression, regression, projection, introjection, the complex and other psychological terms are becoming recognized by almost all psychological researchers as indicating ways in which people react to certain experiences or stimuli in life. Pastoral psychology, having accepted these terms for these psychic reactions, investigates the various ways of solving the inner conflict; in each case there is a particular type of reaction, which is organically connected with the individual conditions and way of life of the person. The heading 'biblical morphology of the solution to the psychic conflict,' then, points to the many ways of realizing the one possible solution to the problem of the inner conflict.

In accordance with that heading we shall proceed to a psychological analysis of certain biblical texts which, in their significant structure, exemplify the solution to the psychic conflict as the terms of Orthodox soteriology define it.

THE 'SCAPEGOAT'

The conscious or unconscious tendency of a guilty person to repress his guilt and to 'project' or 'transfer' it on to another individual has been characterized in psychotherapeutic practice as the 'scapegoat complex'.[2] Moreover, common sense and simple observation of people's reactions in everyday human relations bear witness to the tendency of a guilty person to react in this way. To deny or reject personal guilt by projecting it on to the 'person' of another individual is usually man's easiest way of trying to escape from the oppressive burden of this guilt.

The 'scapegoat complex' must originally be connected with the structure and archetypal functioning of the 'Adam complex.' Man's tendency to shift his personal responsibilities on to the back or shoulders of someone else is organically connected with the psychodynamic reactions 'inherited' from his ancestor, adamic man. Just as Adam's *immediate* solution to the problem of his psychic conflict was to project his guilt upon the person of his wife and upon God, so every descendant of this first man casts off his conflict with himself (that is, his guilty conscience) by the direct reflex method of denying (repressing) his personal guilt and attributing responsibility for the guilt to some other individual who is a 'suitable' recipient. That is to say, a relationship always exists between the guilty person and the 'scapegoat' which facilitates this attribution of responsibility.

The parallel with the 'Adam complex' gives a negative character to the scapegoat complex — that is, resolving the psychic conflict by means of the scapegoat complex appears at first to be a negative solution. But a negative 'disposal' of the psychic conflict is never the authentic solution. Indeed in psychotherapeutic practice the scapegoat complex is seen as an illegitimate solution to man's conflict with his personal or existential guilt. Now this means that the negative version of the scapegoat complex is simply a particular form of expression of the basic psychic conflict. But this complex has a positive aspect as well, which removes its complusive character and hence its functioning as a complex. The positive aspect of the scapegoat complex constitutes the 'type' of the authentic solution to man's inner conflict with his personal or existential guilt. The ritual practice of placing the sins of the Israelites upon the head of the 'scapegoat' (Lev 16.8-10, 21-22, 26) has this meaning.

As we know, according to the texts in Leviticus, the High Priest performs the 'sin offering,' which refers to the cleansing of the people from their sins, in the following way. He takes 'from the congregation of the children of Israel two kinds of goats as a sin offering' (Lev 16.5), which he sets 'before the Lord at the door of tabernacle of meeting.' One of them, the 'scapegoat' is to be an atonement for the sins of the people. 'Aaron shall lay both his hands on the head of the live goat, confess over it all the iniquities of the children of Israel, and all their transgressions, concerning all their sins, putting them on the head of the goat, and shall send it away into the wilderness by the hand of a suitable man' (v. 21). There the scapegoat was thrown to his death over a precipice by the Israelite who took him there. By this act of destruction it was believed that the sins of the people which the scapegoat had taken on his head were also 'destroyed.'

This sacrificial rite of the 'scapegoat' aimed at helping sinful man to resolve his conflict with his guilty conscience in a legitimate way. This way consisted of: a) *Objectifying* the sin. The repression of the guilt which arises from personal sins naturally leads to pushing the sin into the unconscious region of the personality and hence to denying its reality. The Levitican 'sin offering' of the scapegoat is aimed at making sin more conscious as 'alien' to the nature of the human 'body.' The man is not the sin. Sin has 'personal' existence in some way. Sinful man, then, should be able to throw off this alien body of sin and be freed from its destructive consequences. b) Developing a *dialogue* between the sinner and the sin. The sinner can be aware of the existence of sin only when he 'sees into its eyes,' when he looks it 'straight in the face.' The whole formal process of the Levitical ritual facilitates this dialogue of the sinner with sin and strengthens his awareness of it.

Besides these two biomatic (psychological) elements in the sacrifice of the scapegoat there are the 'co-workers' for awareness and dialogue. The High Priest and the scapegoat are the instruments for objectifying sin and developing a dialogue with it. Sinful man is made aware that in order to expel sin he needs the *mediation* of a religious authority and the sacrifice of a suitable recipient of the sin which is to be destroyed. These elements make the sinner aware of his inability to be released from sin by his own efforts alone. He cannot be 'cleansed' from sin on his own. He needs help from a souce outside himself.

The *destruction* (sacrifice) of the scapegoat puts the final seal of certainty on sinful man's release from sin.

This procedure of sacrificing the scapegoat is a solution to man's conflict with his guilty conscience which corresponds to the psychological character of his personality. This means that the Mosaic Law, the 'tutor to bring us to Christ' (Gal 3,24) prepares man's psychologically' (and spiritually) to accept the essentially redemptive way of liberation from the sin by which he is possessed. The sacrifice of the scapegoat has a clearly *typological* character, which confirms its legitimacy as a solution to man's conflict with his guilty conscience. Thus the Mosaic projection of this sacrifice has only a positive character, whereas the disclosure of the 'scapegoat complex' by psychological research and therapeutic practice underlines the negative role which the unconscious repression of guilt and its 'projection' upon some other individual play in the development of interpersonal relations.

So the positive and simultaneously negative aspects of the scapegoat complex present it, on the one hand, as an *authentic solution* to the psychic conflict insofar as this complex 'functions' in accordance with the soteriological terms of the redemption in Christ, and on the other hand, as a *false solution* insofar as it expresses unconscious-obsessive reactions on the part of the guilty person. This simultaneously positive and negative function of the scapegoat complex facilitates still further the positive solution of the psychic conflict. For the positive solution, in accordance with the terms of Orthodox soteriology, is lived not only as man's *conscious* need to put his guilt on the shoulders of a redeemer, but also as an *unconscious* tendency for man's guilty conscience to seek its peace in the personal accountability of the neighbor. This bipolarity of the scapegoat complex reminds us of Caruso's right observation that neurosis has not only a negative character. The neurotic complex really shows the deepest need which a man in conflict with himself (his conscience) has for redemption, for a substantial (genuine) restoration of moral and spiritual balance in the inner world of his psyche.

The pastoral perspective in the case of a person who is under the compulsive pressure of the scapegoat complex must be to try to help him become aware of the psychological mechanism of this complex. This is not always an easy undertaking, just because the scapegoat complex, as an expression of man's deepest need for release from his personal (or existential) guilt, is at the same time a testimony of his 'moral nobility' (Caruso). It is a fact that a morally dead or numbed person is not interested in hiding his guilt or 'transferring' or 'shifting' it to another person. Only a living, moral person reacts with the immediacy of a reflex to the 'troubles' of his wounded conscience. For this reason *resistance* to awareness of personal guilt is a reasonable reaction on the part of a person who finds himself under the constant pressure of the scapegoat complex. The pastoral dialogue in this case should function as a methodical confrontation of the mechanism of general psychic resistance to bringing unconscious processes to consciousness.

THE PRODIGAL SON (Lk 15.11-32)

The parable of the Prodigal Son or the Compassionate Father[4] presents in many images all the stages of development of the basic psychic conflict as we have outlined it so far. Therefore the text of this parable really constitute the whole Gospel of Christ compressed into the meanings contained in these images.

Here too the starting-point of the inner conflict appears in the Prodigal Son's claiming the right to realize his existential prospect in a setting of complete personal *self-efficiency*.[5] He wants to be the one who must, or has the *right* to be 'far' from the authority and house of his father. He has absolute confidence in himself and in his powers to develop his 'portion of goods' in a positive way. He does not think that the existential prospect necessarily has to be realized in the framework of any predetermined procedure. Above all he does not accept the image of existence which has survived 'for ages' in the traditional life of his father's home. The Prodigal Son wants something more totally new, something original, which is required by the new ways of life of his time. This is why he cuts off every tie and every relationship with the traditional existential outlook and 'journeys to a far country.'

This symbolic journey of the Prodigal Son to a far country of course has the meaning of realizing the aim of life (of the existential prospect) within the framework of a universal freedom. Far from any authority a person is free to shape his life according to his individual ideas about the purpose of his existence. But also far from all authority he tries to realize his individual existential ideal by his own individual powers. Indeed up to a point a person does advance on the basis of his individual (independent) existential program. He is in tune with the demands of his own ideas and lives his life as he wishes and as he visualizes it.

But just at this point the parable equates self-realization, emancipated from all authority, with existential poverty, which has the following main characteristics:

a) *The spending and wasting of psychosomatic powers.* The

Prodigal Son 'journeyed to a far country[6] and there wasted his possessions with prodigal living. But when he had spent all, there arose a great famine in that country, and he began to be in want . . .' (vv. 13-16). The Prodigal Son did not add new portions of goods to those which he had received from his father. He did not then increase the profits, the paternal heritage, nor did he gain any other benefit from the life which he led in the new existential setting of emancipation and 'freedom.' He therefore made a 'loss.'[7]

b) *The failure to satisfy his existential expectations.* The Prodigal Son was aiming to enjoy the wealth which he had 'from the goods.' But this pleasure in the satisfaction of existential lodgings and expectations had a time limit. The enjoyment of the 'used' and 'spent' portion of goods was followed by 'existential hunger.' A severe famine which struck the country to which the 'emancipitated' son had journeyed caused him to run short even of daily food. So the kind of 'freedom' or 'emancipation' which this son had chosen did not lead to the satisfaction of his existential expectations.

c) *The degradation of his personal existence.* The shortage created by the spending and wasting of his father's goods, as well as the severe famine, brought the Prodigal Son down to the level of the 'life' of the swine. So 'he would gladly have filled his stomach with the pods that the swine ate.' He became a 'table companion' of animals and especially of the worst ones with regard to their mode of living and maintenance.

d) *Isolation and alienation from 'constructive' human relations.* For a time the 'emancipated' son, in his state of want, looked for help from his fellow men. But 'no one gave him anything.' So he turned to the 'mercy' of the swine.

These characteristics of the 'new existence' which the Prodigal Son created by the free choice which he made also reveal the psychic conflict which he entered at the very moment of choosing. For as we know, this choice was the starting-point of the 'new life.' What followed afterwards was the result of the choice. Therefore the Prodigal Son was already in conflict with the new existential outlook which he had chosen. That is, he met with difficulties in the new conditions of life brought about by the choice which he had made.

It seems that we can summarize the existential consequences of this choice in three words: *want, loneliness, meaninglessness.* At this point the psychological analyses of E. Fromm coincide with the general lines which describe the biomatic experiences and states of the Prodigal Son. A person emancipated from 'original ties,' according to Fromm, reaches a psychological state which makes him aware of his aloneness and meaninglessness. The freedom which he has sought to gain by his emancipation from his original ties leads to psychological problems which he did not have previously. The 'establishment,' consisting of the original ties, had been a guarantee of existential safety and security.[8] Now the freedom which he enjoys arouses in him a very deep fear as to the possibility of making 'productive' use of it.[9] Thus he becomes inwardly aware of the insecurity of aloneness and meaninglessness in the face of the forces which he must overcome in order to enjoy his freedom 'constructively.'

It is clear that this psychological state, which can be understood as a dangling in the chaos of existence, is organically connected with a strong underlying *guilt.* For, as the 'emancipated' son is fearful whether he will ultimately survive within all these negative conditions of existence, he perceives that the responsibility for the success or failure of his initial choice lies with himself and no one else, nor with the conditions of the new life. It is this feeling of *personal* guilt in the course of the existential drama which prepares the way for *solving* the psychic conflict in a positive way.

The text of the parable of the Prodigal Son proposes *self-examination* as a key to resolving the psychic conflict. The 'emancipated' son, who was at the same time unsuccesful in his existential choice, said . . . 'when he came to himself . . . .' Before proceeding to an evaluation of his personal state, and especially before he perceived the nature of the solution to his existential self, to his authentic individuality. This means that he rejected the false image of himself which had been created for him by his 'new' existential choice, and be became aware of the real situation in which he now found himself. He saw himself as he really was and not as he wanted to be.

From another point of view, this self-examination was an evaluation of his personal state compared to the life he had led previously under the existential outlook set by *paternal* authority. So the 'emancipated' son 'when he came to himself said, "How many of my father's hired servants have bread enough and to spare, and I perish here with hunger." ' (v.17). Within the 'establishment' of the paternal home there was no problem of maintenance. Even the servants have abundant possessions and their life was 'dignified.' This meant that it would pay the Prodigal Son to be a servant in his father's house rather than to eat with the pigs. This evaluation of his personal situation revealed to him a new existential outlook which was easy to realize by returning to his father's house. Therefore the reasoning of his solution to the existential problem followed automatically. 'I will arise and go to my father, and I will say to him, "Father, I have sinned against heaven and before you, and I am no longer worthy to be called your son. Make me like one of your hired servants" ' (vv.18-19).

Indeed this reasoning contains all the elements of an existential outlook which amounts to the solution of the basic conflict. These elements are the following:

a) *Awareness of the unsuccessfulness of choosing a way of life emancipated from the paternal authority.* The Prodigal Son understood his personal life story in a complete series of biomaric experiences (or 'images'). He reached the conclusion given in verses 18-19 after becoming directly *aware*[10] of the development of his existential drama. This awareness of the basic conflict.

b) *Confession of the failure of his existential outlook.* The acceptance by the 'emancipated son' of the fact tht his existential outlook was a failure, and especially his confession of this failure, were likewise essential elements in the authentic solution of the basic inner conflict. Yet it is characteristic of the text of the parable that this confession took place 'in repetition,' first as an exclusively individual experience (as existential reasoning) and afterwards as information or communication to the Father. This repetition in the biblical text certainly underlines the core of the solution to the basic inner conflict. For it is possible to reach the point of awareness without being willing to go on to the *confession* which redeems.

c) *Recognition and acceptance of personal guilt for the failure of his existential outlook.* The confession of the failure of his existential outlook which is contained in the words: 'Father, I have sinned against heaven and before you' underlines at the same time the recognition and acceptance of personal guilt for the failure of this outlook. The 'emancipated' son admitted his guilt and confessed it unreservadly. No justification was forward for his failure to realize the ideal to which he himself in absolute freedom had given preference. Acceptance of personal guilt, without reservations or conditions, is also an essential element in the process of genuinely solving the basic conflict. This acceptance works in the depth of the human personality as a purification, which makes a new choice possible.

d) *Choice of a new existential outlook.* This choice was founded first and foremost on a way of life which acknowledged (absolutely) his unworthiness in connection with the claims of his father's authority. The 'emancipated' and now unsuccessful *son* acknowledged that he could not be worthy child of his father. 'I am no longer worthy to be called your son.' This outlook, that of being a worthy son of his father, seemed to him incompatible with his personal guilt. For this reason the Prodigal Son sought the least that was possible to seek. 'Make me like one of your hired servants.' This was his new existential outlook — to be equal in rank to a servant of his father.

All these constituent elements of the new outlook, which is actually the authentic solution to the psychic conflict, can be summed up in one word of fact, *repentance.* But here the repentance was lived not simply as a change of mind. The unsuccessful son proceeded to make a *sacrifice* which seemed obvious to him. The choice of this particualar new outlook underlines his renunciation of high existential claims. He did not set himself the goal of gaining what he had lost by his emancipation from paternal authority. He was satisfied with a lower existential prospect. *Repentance* as an expression of a spirit of deep humility is a real sacrifice. This sacrifice is the only possibility for solving the basic psychic conflict. A person who is in conflict with himself because of a mistaken existential outlook can be freed from this conflict only by means of a sacrifice.

The psychological (and spiritual) examination of the parable of the Prodigal Son underlines the main structural elements of the basic inner conflict not only as to its origin but also as to its solution. *Repentance* as self-sacrifice[11] is the *only* solution to the basic psychic conflict, as well as to its particular forms. Moreover, a comparison of the findings of depth psychology and psychotherapy with the general lines of the solution to the psychic conflict as sketched in the parable of the Prodigal Son reveal points in common.

Psychotherapy too looks for a 'change of mind' in the neurotic person. After the neurotic has become as fully aware as possible of the structure of his psychic conflict, the aim is that through a sacrifice he should renounce the existential goals which brought him to this conflict. For psychotherapy 'repentance' and 'humility' (of course with differentiated conceptual contents) are *keys* to the cure of a neurotic condition. Inner resistances, arrogant 'attitudes' and adamant 'obsessions' are notions, but they are also functions which oppose the notions and biomatic states of 'repentance,' 'humility' and 'sacrifice.' Therefore in the two cases of therapeutic work the goals coincide: repentance, humility, sacrifice. Only the axiological orientations differ. But if psychotherapy itself succeeds in being healed of its neurosis (Caruso), then it will acknowledge that the psychological channels of *repentance, humility* and *sacrifice* inevitably lead to the Christian meaning of life: to restoring man to his first position: that of a child of God. The neurotic himself who is in psychotherapy is also in search of the 'best robe' (v. 22). But psychotherapy does not know this robe, since it is itself bare of value perspectives. Because it makes the psychological factor absolute, it cannot reach the authentic solution to the psychic conflict. Only the Gospel of Christ can offer such a solution to the neurotic. Pastoral psychology is called to serve this purpose.

THE PUBLICAN

The parable of the Pharisee and the tax collector, or publican, is a description of the *symptoms* of the basic psychic conflict in its two main aspects, negative and positive. An account of the negative aspect has already been given in the preceding chapter with the description and analysis of the symptoms of the symptoms of the conflict presented by the Pharisee's behavior. The image of the tax collector completes the general picture of this conflict as the Lord wishes to give it to us through the spirit of the whole parable.

The main characteristic of the solution (or healing) of the psychic conflict as presented in the publican's behavior is the *absolute* way in which he lives his guilt. This way is reflected, moreover, in the length of the Gospel description. The psychological diagram of the publican's behavior is limited to a single verse in the Gospel text. The publican does not express himself with overabundant words and impressive outward (bodily) display as the Pharisee does. His behavior is *simple*. This simplicity is underlined by the plain prayer: 'God, be merciful to me a sinner.' What the publican has to say is a prayer for forgiveness and mercy. It is this fact which shows that he lives his personal guilt in an absolute way.

The chief characteristic of this way can be indicated as follows:

a) The tax collector lives his guilt *alone*. This means that he does not make comparisons with other men as the Pharisee does. He does not share out his guilt with other sinners. By his whole attitude and behavior he shows that he recognizes his guilt as his own 'exclusive property.'

This attitude of the publican towards his guilt gives the outward impression of *isolation*. The publican lives his guilt 'privately' and this prompts the observer of his behavior to think that he has fallen into a negative sort of *aloneness*. But this idea is undoubtedly mistaken. The 'guilty isolation' of the publican *reveals* the absence of destructive inner conflicts and debasing discord. The publican is not internally divided. He is not in conflict with himself in the sense of *negative*, contradictory inner states. The manner in which he lives his guilt as a process of resolving his inner conflict underlines the inner unity and intergration of his personality. Because the publican has entered upon the path of genuinely resolving his psychic conflict, he has an inner unity which leads him to simplicity[12] of behavior, This simplicity is expressed as a 'guilty isolation' but with a positive character. Therefore the publican neither projects nor 'transfers' his guilt on to other people. He perceives that he is guilty and the responsibility for this guilt lies squarely upon him, and him alone.

b) The publican does not offer *excuses* for his guilt. He confesses it, behaves with a strong sense of guilt, but also (with this sensitivity) he does not attempt to justify his guilt state. This absence of any defence is likewise a symptom of inner (psychic) harmony and integration.

The attempt at self-justification in the course of the 'guilty dialogue' which usually develops in the network of interpersonal relations betrays unconscious processes connected with repressed feelings of guilt. Modern psychology is already clear on this point. The findings emerging from its research into man's guilty reactions in general underline the organic (unconscious) connection between these feelings and attempts at self-defence or self-justification. Moreover, in the spiritual experience of Orthodox asceticism an *absolute* admission of personal guilt is considered a step towards perfection. Therefore the behavior of the publican is an expression of inner unity and integration. That is, the absence of any excuses for his guilty state confirms that the *living* of guilt is an *absolutely* conscious experience and does not express unconscious guilty processes. The publican does not repress his guilt, he does not offer excuses for it. This guilty reaction is a fundamental element in the authentic solution of the psychic conflict.

c) The publican *attacks* himself in the sense of a 'psychosomatic self-affirmation of his guilt. The admission of guilt can of course be an internal and secret personal experience. But to live it wholly and personally demands somatic evidence of this admission as well. This is how we must understand the (positive) guilty reaction of the publican who 'beat his breast' as he prayed to God.

This detail in the description of the publican's guilty behavior is highly significant, precisely because it confirms that the publican is living his guilt wholly — not only inwardly but outwardly as well. The publican's way of living his guilt might have been limited to his inner psychic world, but that kind of guilt reaction would have left room for the formation of a 'somatic' mask of virtue and righteousness. While it often happens that a guilty person understands and admits his guilt, in his bodily expression and movements he tries to maintain (consciously or unconsciously?) the dignity of a righteous person. But this already indicates an effort to conceal his guilty state and therefore a tendency to repress the guilt. The tax collector wants not only to feel his guilty state palpably by beating his breast, but also to declare it and expose it openly to the eyes of other men.

d) The tax collector keeps the eyes of his mind fixed on his inner world. In contrast to the Pharisee, who is steadily concentrated on the outer world, from which he expects recognition of his 'superiority,' the publican 'would not so much as raise his eyes to heaven.' The position of his head emphasizes the absolute interiorization of the problem of personal guilt. This indicates that the publican is not seeking the solution to his guilt problem in the outer world with which he 'has dealings.' Furthermore, he prefers to meet God not in the 'material' heaven of the outer world but in the abysmal chaos of his guilty state. Here too it is a question of a 'circular motion of the mind' which is absolutely justified. For the supplication 'God be merciful to me a sinner' is more genuine and more spontaneous when it comes from within the chaos of this guilty state.

The emphasis on the basic characteristics of the publican's way of living his guilt as seen in his behavior is at the same time a description of the authentic way of solving the basic conflict from the point of view of the Gospel. That is, if man's primary psychic conflict is maintained and stirred up by an unconscious yet strong guilt anxiety, the best way to resolve it is to make this anxiety *conscious* and to cure it with the help of a *redeemer*.

But the solution to the inner conflict in the image of the guilty publican can be understood better as a whole if it is compared with the image of the neurotic of our time and his psychotherapeutic encounter. This man is exhausted by the turmoil of experiences and therefore his basic request (whether he knows it or not) is to be freed from these experiences. The tragic error of psychotherapy is just that it does not recognize the real (moral) character of the turmoil of guilt in the neurotic person. It considers the guilt experiences as psychological conflicts without any other axiological evaluation. But precisely because the experiences of guilt are upsetting the neurotic person they always have incalculable existential depth, and this requires therapeutic confrontation in the framework of *universal* values. This framework is described in condensed form in the image of the tax collector praying with deep humility.

Finally, the general result of this study of the guilty image of

the publican can be summed up in the idea that the only positive
solution to the basic psychic conflict which arises and is maintained and functions by the power of guilt experiences is *absolute* acceptance of personal guilt. For this means that the person in conflict with himself *denies* the false image of himself and in this way
purifies and breaks down his *compensation* for the 'likeness,' which
the conflict is about, as he tries to be faithful to the demands of
the sublime hope of deification. As soon as the neurotic acknowledges
his errors or wrong evaluations, he is on his way towards the right
solution of his existential problem. Insofar as he is in a position
to *surrender* both his personal and his existential guilt into the hands
of the true redeemer with the prayer 'God be merciful to me a sinner,' he experiences the justification of the publican. He is restored
to the 'original beauty' in the sense of justification.

THE PARALYTIC OF CAPERNAUM (Mt 9.2-7; Mk 2.1-2; Lk 5.18-24)

The gospel narrative about the miraculous healing of the
paralytic of Capernaum puts before us the image of a psychic conflict which has manifest somatic consequences.

As we know, the Lord healed a paralyzed man with the words
'Your sins are forgiven.' In this event there are perhaps three things
to be distinguished: first the Lord's miraculous action, which in itself
is beyond any criticism or debate; secondly, the expressive 'instrument' of healing, the Lord's words, which 'provoke' the bystanders;
and thirdly, the paralyzed man, or more particularly his illness. It
is essential to distinguish these three aspects of the gospel narrative
if we are to isolate its 'human' elements and above all to see the
function of the human presuppositions which are indispensable for
the accomplishment of the soteriological work of the Church.

It is true that linking sins with physical ailments always pro-
vokes the sceptical reader. Anyone who has not an unshakable faith
in the truth of the Gospel is scandalized when he reads the familiar
text about the healing of a chronic paralysis with the words 'Your
sins are forgiven.' The rationalist in particular rejects out of hand
a causal relationship between sin and physical illness. He cannot
understand how it is possible that a 'spiritual' (or moral) action
could result in such a chronic and incurable bodily sickness.

Contemporary psychology and psychotherapy have 'healed' the

infirmity of this understanding by explaining the hysterical symptom. As we know, systematic clinical study of the hysterical phenomenon has been going on since the time of Freud, and it has led to the general conclusion that this phenomenon is *psychologenic.* According to the findings of depth psychology and psychotherapy, hysteria is a product of unconscious processes. In particular, strong repressions of unpleasant experiences lead to an unhealthy psychic and somatic state which is now characterized as conversion neurosis. As Rudolf Brun says, 'conversion'[13] is the name given to the ability of the personality to release his repressed emotional states into the somatic sphere. But of course it is not simply a question of experiences which have a purely psychological meaning and character. In the case of conversion these emotional states (effects) are the biomatic core of a psychic conflict. This is also what Vera Scheffen[14] brings out in her special study based on clinical material, emphasizing that the sufferer from an organ neurosis is unaware of his inner conflicts, which he is trying to solve by the somatic path. This particular reaction of the neurotic, to escape into somatic illness in order (in an unconscious way) to solve a severe inner conflict, has already been characterized as 'escape into illness' (Grunewald). So conversion neurosis is an expression, on the part of a person with a severe conflict, of a desire to be freed from the pressure and mental burden brought about by this conflict.

But what is this burden of the psychic conflict? The answer is not hard to find if one combines and finally sums up the partial conclusions of research on the hysterical phenomenon which have been formulated from Freud's time to the present day. This burden is the wounded conscience.[15] A person who expresses a severe inner conflict by paralysis wants to be freed from intolerable feelings of guilt. This general conclusion drawn by modern psychology and psychotherapy is enough to convince even the rationalist observer of the paralytic of Capernaum that the Lord dealt with him primarily in terms of the human causes of his disease.[16]

As far as the paralytic of Capernaum is suffering because of his sins, he can really be regarded as a type of 'neurotic' person, that is, one who suffers bodily because he has repressed a severe and all-embracing experience. Certainly at this point a distinction can be admitted between the *direct* and *indirect* consequences of sin. In the present case the paralysis may be a natural consequence of the body's having participated in committing a sin. For instance, as we know, an immoral life can lead to 'paralysis.' But also the repression of guilt which comes from committing sin in another area of existence (that is, without direct participation of the body) can lead to the same result. In both cases, however, the essential thing is that sin, as the root of the intolerable experience of guilt, can result in organ neurosis among other things.

The psychological problem in the 'mechanism' of organ neurosis is how to make the patient aware of his repressed guilt. This problem is difficult to solve because the hysterical neurotic cannot accept that the source of his illness is guilt. He is sure that since he is suffering physically, the cause of the illness is physical.[17] So he cannot understand the direct, causal relationship between personal guilt and bodily illness. But the problem is not limited to this inability. For, since the neurotic state is essentially a complex psychic condition, even if the neurotic achieves awareness of his repressed guilt, he still has other problems to face. These problems concern the possibility of a *change* in his attitude towards the basic purposes of existence. The fundamental question here is the purposes of existence. The fundamental question here is following: How far is the neurotic person capable of changing his basic existential orientation and accepting a new existential outlook?

Therefore the psychological problem involved in the cure of organ neurosis can be formulated along these main lines: a) the necessity of becoming *aware* of the primary psychic conflict; b) the necessity of *understanding* the repression of guilt as the cause which generates the conflict; c) the necessity of changing one's existential orientation (through admitting personal guilt); and, d) the necessity of a long-term *struggle* to fulfill the new purposes of existence.

But the solution to this complex psychological (existential) problem is not so obvious as one would think. While the prognosis is good from one point of view, from another there may be disappointment. This means that while in theory the existential problem of the neurotic seems easy to solve (through awareness), in practice there are incomparable difficulties.

The gravest difficulty is usually in the neurotic's inability to go on to apply practically the new ideas which emerge from the awareness of his existential problem. The neurotic must *understand* his difficult position and *want* to change it. But the greatest problem is that of his *ability* to want to change his existential direction and his *incapacity* ro go ahead and make the change. Therefor most often the neurotic is able to advance to the point where he says: I *want* to but I *cannot!* I see the reality but I cannot change it.

In this state the neurotic hopes for hjelp from someone else (the psychotherapist?) or 'help from on high.' Psychologically this means that while perhaps he understands his problem to a certain degree, he has a passive attitude towards it. This passive attitude probably alternates with 'desperate' attempts which do not bear fruit because they are not in harmony with the fundamental change which he must make: a change of mind. He must change his mind in the sense of renouncing the old 'world,' and this involves also the search for a new world, a 'new creation.'

Although, as we have said, we cannot understand logically the texture and framework of the miracle of the Lord's healing of the paralytic, we can perhaps comprehend in what area of his personality the miraclous act intervened. That is to say, the paralytic is not excluded from belonging to the category of those reaction is: 'I want to but I cannot.' He wanted to be healed and he understood that this healing had to take place in the setting of a rebirth, but he did no have the power to lift himself to the biomatic level required for this rebirth. With the assurance: 'Your sins are forgiven,' the Lord helped the paralytic to live through all the stages of his healing. He encouraged[18] him in the good intentions of his good self to overcome the resistance of his sinful self. The assurance that his sins were forgiven was equivalent to the assurance: you have been freed of your guilt. But deliverance from the burden of guilt automatically implies undoing the psychosomatic 'knot' which is expressed by the paralysis.

This psychological examination of the healing of the paralytic does not have the meaning of 'annuling' the redemption. Miracles can never be rationalized. But the typological character of the miracle is clear here too. Its soteriological meaning is summed up in the general conclusion that even organic diseases can be cured by freeing

the person from guilt.[19] Modern psychotherapy accepts this conclusion because it is also validated by clinical experience. But apart
from this fact, there is an essential difference between Christian
and psychotherapeutic redemption. Whereas psychotherapeutic
redemption is *formal* (it works or should work 'in accordance with
the Christ archetype'), Christian redemption is the *sole* authentic
solution to the neurotic psychosomatic knot.

Therefore the solution of a psychic conflict which is also expressed somatically (as an organ neurosis) is directly connected
with the person's release from guilt. Any other attempt to heal
or *compensate* the organ inferiorities which arise from entangle-
ment in problems of guilt is a 'false solution.' The healing of the
paralytic of Capernaum anticipates modern psychotherapy and
gives the sound solution to the problem of dealing with the
hysterical phenomenon, i.e. conversion neurosis.

ZACCHAEUS (LK. 19.1-10)

The case of the 'restitution' and 'conversion' of Zacchaeus offers a solution to the psychic conflict in the form of *material* repara-
tion for the consequences of his guilt towards society as a whole.
This of course does not mean that Zacchaeus has not previously
gone through the stages essential to a positive solution of the
psychic conflict. Nevertheless the reader of the gospel passage is
struck by Zacchaeus's readiness and eagerness to proceed to a
generous sacrifice of his material goods and of his property in
general. Apart from the fact that this sacrifice is a material one,
it expresses and confirms the change or renewal of the existential
outlook of Zacchaeus, the chief tax collector. Up to this moment
the central aim of his existence has been to collect and acquire
money and material goods in general, and now 'suddenly' this goal
is discarded and replaced by the request for a restoration of relationships of fairness and love with other people. What interests
Zacchaeus from now on is the healing of injustices to his fellow
men which he has commited in the past. This is why, instead of
reacting in another way to the unexpected visit of Jesus to his home,
he goes on to say 'I give half of my goods to the poor' and makes
the other 'half' available for liberally making good the injustices
which he has commited 'wittingly' or 'unwittingly.'

Despite the fact that again in the case of Zacchaeus the gospel description is brief and limited to very general lines, still it gives us all the main indications of a psychological (and spiritual) reaction which has to do with man's guilt problem. Thus in Zacchaeus's case too we can 'construct' the diagram of his reaction, beginning with the *external* characteristics of his behavior. For unseen (unconscious) psychic process can only be understood if a careful study is made of the sequence and components of the reactions of the human personality.

First of all, the brevity of the description projects the change in Zacchaeus's 'guilty behavior' as a *sudden* psychological reaction. To the naive mind this means that the actual confession of his guilt is a psychological (and spiritual) event for which Zacchaeus was not prepared. But today it is well known that unconscious process always precede the outward reactions of the human personality. A *sudden conversion* is phenomenologically sudden. From the point of view of its origin it has been developing for an indeterminate period of time. Hence in the case of Zacchaeus we cannot accept that the offer of his property as an expression of his guilty self-consciousness arises out of the emotion of the moment. It may be that Zacchaeus himself does not know what he has been harbouring up to this moment as an inner (psychic) conflict. For his psychological reaction to Jesus's visit to his home comes from the seat of his primary psychic conflict. And indeed it is a reaction which manifests the solution of the conflict. Zacchaeus behaves with absolute freedom. He detaches himself from his material goods with the ease which his inner freedom and *simplicity* give him. This freedom and the simplicity of his behavior, which at the same time expresses the dimensions of a new existential outlook, underlines the absence of inner (psychic) discords and conflicts. Zacchaeus is not acting under the pressure of conflicts and contradictory psychic states. The fact that he puts his material existence, and certainly also his emotional wealth, *completely* at the disposal of his fellow men manifests his inner wholeness. Through expressing an *all-embracing* personal sacrifice, Zacchaeus stands before Jesus as an integrated personality.

A general outline of the psychological (and spiritual) course of Zacchaeus's 'sudden' conversion can be drawn up then as follows:

a) *Unconscious living of a psychological process, preparation, conversion.* During this time Zacchaeus 'meets' psychologically stimuli from the outer world which fertilize these inner processes. b) *Conquest of Zacchaeus's personality by the unconscious processes.* His 'identification' with the repressed guilt complex reaches its peak and by the law of *enantiodroma* his direction is reversed, leading him to awareness of his guilt. c) *Living in the framework of a 'guilt conflict' of the need for conversion.* Under the pressure of his conflict, Zacchaeus seeks Jesus out. His desire to 'see who Jesus was' (Lk.19,3) does not express 'pure' curiosity, but an irresistable ('compulsive') inner prompting. d) *Breaking through of the need for conversion, sparked by Jesus's words 'Zacchaeus, make haste and come down, for today I must stay at your house'* (v.5). Zacchaeus's meeting with Jesus in his family home contributes decisively to the collapse of all his concious or unconscious resistance to the need to actualize the conversion. e) *Actual confession and expression of his personal guilt, as the solution to the guilth conflict.* The confession of guilt and the material restitution for the consequences of this guit, together with the offer of love for the poor, define the dimensions and nature of the solution to this psychic conflict. f) *Living in freedom of the spirit.* The Lord's assurance: 'Today salvation has come to this house' confirms the solution of Zacchaeus's psychic (guilt) conflict. This means that Zacchaeus now lives in the *innocence* and *simplicity* of the publican, that is, in genuine freedom of the spirit.

In Zacchaeus's case the particular element to which attention will have to be given is that in order for these unconsious processes leading to a *constructive* solution to the psychic conflict to break through to a positive fulfilment, what was needed was *sparking* rather than a 'scholastic' dialogue. The dialogue of glances between Zacchaeus and Jesus was more fruitful than any verbal dialogue. The Lord, confining himself to this dialogue, calls Zacchaeus to come down from the sycamore and to receive him in his home. The absence of any 'incriminating 'dialogue' between Jesus and Zacchaeus could support the notion of sparking. This means that the deeper and more severe we suspect the psychic conflict to be, the more limited should be the incriminating dialogue with the person under pastoral care. In the effort to resolve a a conflict sparking is usually more effective than a dialogue of the 'catechetical instruction' type.

Finally, it is obvious that in using the term 'sparking' we have in mind the *limiting* of the incriminating dialogue or its *biomatic* function to the framework of a *challenge*. By his silence and his glance the Lord called forth Zacchaeus's expression and manifestation of repentance, and indeed in a spontaneous manner. He neither accused nor taught Zacchaeus. Since the latter was psychologically (and morally) ready to acknowledge his guilt and proceed to make good the material consequences of it, he was offered the spark to set off his guilt reaction.

Zacchaeus is an example of a guilty person who, having advanced to the psychological process of a positive solution of his inner conflict, is waiting for the spark which will help him to complete and actualize this solution.

GENERAL CONCLUSIONS

In this handbook the chief aim of our examination of the problem of the basic psychic conflict has been to give a general sketch of the *structure* and *functioning* of the conflict. This general examination of man's fundamental existential problem can serve as the lens through which every problem which is clearly in the nature of conflict can be studied and confronted pastorally. As we have seen, a number of problems of the human personality can be traced back to their *original* roots or starting-points if we view them in the light of the primary psychic conflict. Pastoral problems, as we know, have a more manifestly existential character, especially in cases where they are directly linked with the individual's existential outlook. The problem, after this sketch of the structure and function of the primary psychic conflict, is to see how the pastor can make constructive use of the material in this handbook. So we shall now present diagrammatically the framework of the main approach by which we can examine a number of pastoral problems that have the character of a secondary psychic conflict.

1) Every problem of the human personality has two aspects, an *outer* and an *inner* one. The first aspect relates to the 'phenomenal' psychic events or circumstances. The second aspect is hidden by the veil of the unconscious.

2) The external features or elements of the problem are usually characterized (when viewed in the light of the psychic conflict) as *symptoms.*

3) The *symptom* is not the conflict itself, but betrays and reveals the conflict. In this case the *symptom* is the door through which, if we go properly, we come to the seat of the inner conflict.

132

4) The problem of the human personality is always that he lives a life of guilt. As we have seen, this statement has a firm theological basis. But modern psychology (as psychotherapy) finds that this problem comes within the scope of its own anthropological and scientific structure as well.

5) Every person is squeezed in the clash between what he should become (or be) and what he is. The primary psychic conflict works as a counterpoise between the 'given' capabilities of the human personality and the command to realize the 'likeness.' This dynamic counterpoise constitutes the problem of man's existential outlook.

6) Man's existential outlook is organically joined with his existential guilt.

7) In every pastoral problem existential and personal guilt live (in the same existential core) as concentric circles. From *personal* guilt we are led to existential and vice versa. Every 'trivial' problem (with the character of a conflict) leads us to the nature and character of the existential guilt. Moreover, existential guilt helps us to understand the 'monstrous' existential dimensions of the 'trivial' problem.

8) The *solution* to the pastoral problem must be connected in the first instance with the awareness and acceptance of existential and personal guilt.

Diagram of the 'complex' of primary and secondary psychic conflicts, based on the principles of concentric circles.

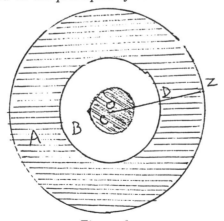

Figure 1.

A = (circular) area of the primary psychic conflict.

B = (circular) area of the secondary psychic conflict.

C = The common core of both conflicts.

OZ:OD = The ray OZ belongs to the circular area of the existential outlook (or of the primary psychic conflict), and in relation to the ray OD it defines the difference in existential dimentions between the two psychic conflicts (primary and secondary).

Note. The circular field of the primary psychic conflict (A) coincides with the 'dimensions' of the existential outlook.

On the basis of these general concluding principles, in what follows we shall undertake a probable estimate of the root causes or factors involved in a pastoral problem which has the manifest character of a psychic conflict.

Mr X is an educated man of forty. He is well established professionally, and this means that he is not faced with financial problems. He is a good Christian and is eager to see his family progress in the Christian life. He is the father of two children in primary school.

One day during his confession to his spiritual father he complains that signs of 'temperamental incompatibility' are appearing in his relationship with his wife. Their dissensions often start from insignificant matters and expand into psychological states which are a threat to the peace of the family. He assures his spiritual father that he himself does what he can to prevent the disagreements with his wife from coming to a head. But she is unyielding. She is arrogant. 'She knows everything." She never accepts an idea or opinion which is contrary to her own. She always wants to have the last word . . .[1]

This situation, as Mr. X says, distresses him and he points out that with conditions as they are, he cannot note any progress from the point of view of Christian spiritual endeavour. Indeed he understands that his own nervous irritation has recently been intensified to the point where it makes him more touchy and less capable of dialogue with his wife even on subjects unrelated to disagreements and differences of opinion.

Therefore he suggests that his spiritual father should 'speak' to his wife and emphasize to her the need to restore marital harmony in the family, which is indispensable for the sake of the children's psychological development.

The confessor accepts Mr. X's suggestion, telling him that he will form his full opinion on the problem and give it to him after his conversation with the wife.

In her meeting with the confessor, Mr. X's wife in her turn complains about her husband's 'dictatorial' character. He is absolute in his ideas, she declares, and he wants to assert his authority over her willy-nilly in order to have his own way in the home. When she offers to have a dialogue with him in a spirit of 'equality' and recognition of indiviual 'dignity' he accuses her of anti-familial feminism and incorrigible arrogance. She adds that she is astonished that he has presented their marital disagreements to the spriritual father in such a way as to humiliate her. She is sure that this will make their relationship still more difficult.

The confessor is faced with a familiar and 'typical' problem of marital relations which is characterized as 'temperamental incompatibility.' This expression is usually used to declare that two marriage partners do not 'match' because their characters are not 'in harmony.' They have opposite ways of behaving and reaching within the space which they share as a couple and a family. Their contrasting ways of behaving lead them into 'conflicts' which show that they cannot 'co-exist' in the same living space.

The confessor is now faced with a pastoral problem. Two good Christians (since they make confession and attend church) marriage partners are in 'conflict' within their family life. He is supposed to be a catalyst for healing this conflict. How will he reason out this problem?

General pastoral perspective. Actually disharmony of characters is more often a sign that they conflict because of a *similarity* in their ways of reacting. It is usually similar characters which conflict. Therefore in typical cases of 'temperamental incompatibility' we have a collision between two people with the same dispositional tendency. In everyday parlance one would speak of a 'clash of two *egoisms.*

Diagram of the 'conflict' projection of the symptom.

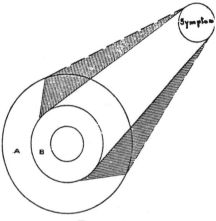

Figure 2.

Symptom = 'temperamental incompatibility.'
A = (circular) area of the psychic conflict.
B = (circular) area of the secondary psychic conflict.
The symptom is a 'conflict' projection not only of the secondary psychic conflict (fictitious image of the 'good' spouse), but all of the primary psychic conflict (fictious image of the 'likeness').

The mutual accusations of absolute opinions, unyielding attitudes and dictatiorial dispositions really confirm the clash of two egoistic 'resistances' to the development of an interpersonal relationship. So the mutual accusations, and particualarly the imputation to the other (spouse) of egoistic, arrogant behavior, are a *symptom* of a collision between two personalities. Yet at the same time, in accordance with what we have presented so far in this handbook, they are also a *symptom* of an inner conflict in the one who accuses the other of direct *aggression* (tendency to 'impose' upon the other) or indirect aggression ('psychic resistance,' 'lack of spiritual pliability or humility').

This symptom leads us straight to the nature and area of the primary psychic conflict, whereby there is opposition in the individual between his real state (what he is at a given moment) and his idealized self-image, which he wants unsullied and unchallenged. 'Sensitiveness' and egoism have a *direct* reference and relation

to the *idealized* and *fictitious* image which every person has formed of himself. This image is the *mask*, which 'protects' the authentic
image of the person's existential outlook, that is, in our case, the
'likeness'! Everyone wants to have and to keep a good idea of
himself. This reassures him (in an unconscious way) that he is in
harmony with the totality of the demands of the 'likeness.'' That
is, he *is* as he *should* be. But every doubt or assault on this 'as
he should be' (i.e., the idealized personal image) evokes the individual's resistance or aggression against the doubter or assailant.

Why? Because the *ultimate* substratum of human psychic life
is being challenged, and this opens the way for *guilt anxiety*. So
in the oppositions aroused by a conflict of like (egoistic) characters,
the deepest psychodynamic motive, acting autonomously and by
reflex, is repressed existential guilt. But as we have said, since this
guilt coincides with personal guilt, like two concentric circles, the
existential guilt adds fuel to the personal guilt, and the 'trivial'
discord which is the start of a marital dialogue is very easily
heightened to a 'clash' of characters.

The resolution of the conflict can only be brought about after
both partners go back psychologically to the *guilty* depth of their
reactions. Recognition of the guilty starting-point of their reactions can ease the difficulties of the *marital dialogue*. The ability,
that is, to admit their *possible* or *probable* weaknesses or failings
brings their idealized image closer to their real state and does away
with their *aggressive* reactions as far as possible. In this way the
psychodynamic tension of the clash of temperaments is relieved,
or coexistence and living together in the same field of action and
life is made easier.

If we compare the coexistence or living together of existential
and personal guilt with two concentric circles, it is easier to understand the *organic* relation between the primary (original) conflict
and the secondary psychic conflict, which is fed by guilt from the
same existential core (the same 'center'). In the case we gave as
an example the original conflict is the conflict which the partners
as independent individuals experience when they confront the 'likeness.' The secondary conflict is in the way each relates to the image of the partner. Each wants to be a 'good' spouse. Attacking
or questioning this image arouses guilt reactions which present

an inexhaustible symptomatology.

Our example, then, confirms: a) the primary psychic conflict; b) the secondary psychic conflict; c) the 'symptom' of a psychic conflict ('temperamental incompatibility') and d) the *aggressive* reaction as an expression of guilt belonging to the psychic conflict in general, which is fed psychodynamically from the same 'center' of conflict.

Of course, beyond these basis psychodynamic elements of a pastoral problem, the pastor who has a richer psychological education is in a position to note others as well, analyzing more deeply the psychological connections of the symptom with the secondary and primary psychic conflicts. For instance, a study of the reaction of every spouse in relation to the family environment out of which he came can produce more elements which will give a broader interpretation to and explain more clearly the *depth* and *dimensions* of the temperamental incompatibility of the partners. But for the present, the elements which we have already indicated (the primary psychic conflict, the symptom, the secondary conflict, the existential outlook, existential guilt and personal guilt) serve for examining the pastoral problem in such a way that the *general* lines of the course of its solution can be defined. This was the purpose of this first book on pastoral psychology. The material of the second book should offer more possibilities for determining this path, always, of course, in terms of the necessary contribution of the human factor to the work of man's spiritual fulfilment and salvation.

NOTES

INTRODUCTION

[1]*Theology*, vol. 22 (1951) no. 4 and vol. 23 (1952) no. 1 (in Greek).

[2]Ibid. 23 (1952) no. 1, p. 59.

[3]Ibid. 22 (1951) no. 4, p. 197.

[4]As Erich Fromm observes, the theory of the unconscious motive of man's behavior created a new basis for critical thinking. 'Before Freud it was considered sufficient to know a man's conscious intentions in order to judge his sincerity. After Freud this was no longer enough; in fact, it was very little. Behind consciousness lurked the hidden reality, the unconscious, which was the key to man's real intentions.' Erich Fromm, *The crisis of Psychoanalysis*, (London 1971), p. 14.

[5]Pierre, Daco, *Les prodigieuses victoires de la psychologie moderne* (Verviers, Belgium 1960), p. 11.

[6]'There are cases in which the person who appears to be fulfilling a commandment of Christ, in reality is motivated by passion. Through his evil thought he thus destroys a good deed.' Introduction to the 200 texts on the spiritual law by Mark the Ascetic (Thessalonike 1974), p. 38 (in Greek).

[7]A. J. Mason, *Fifty spiritual homilies of St. Makarius the Egyptian* (London 1921), pp. 265 and 311 (PG 34.768C, 820C).

[8]Ibid. p. 302 (PG 34.809D).

[9]Oskar Pfister, *Das Christentum und die Angst* (Zurich 1944).

[10]Here an objection might be raised to our 'construing' of the parables. But inasmuch as the parables were 'constructed' by the Lord, the knower of man *par excellence*, their existential 'immediacy' is obviously assured. The psychological types in the parables are genuine from every human point of view.

[11]Archimandrite Elias Mastroyannopoulos, *The Fathers of the Church and Man* (Athens), pp. 277 (in Greek).

[12]James H. Leuba, *The Psychology of Religious Mysticism* (New York 1925). Herbert Grabet, *Die ekstatischen Erlebnisse der Mystiker und Psychopathen* (Stuttgart 1929). Alois Mager, *Mystik als seelische Wirklichkeit. Eine Psychologie des mystischen Bewusstsein* (Bremen 1951). Evelyn Underhill, *Mysticism. A Study in the Nature and Development of Man's Spiritual Consciousness* (London 1960).

[13]C. G. Jung, *Symbolism of the spirit*, Collected works vol. 11, pp. 174 and 190.

[14]The case of the Roman Catholic theologian, physician and psychologist Marc

Oraison is certainly characteristic. He proposed combining the clinical observations of sexual life with the theoretical positions of Christian teaching in order to get a 'theology of sexuality.' He considered that such a theology would show us that sexuality in the universe is an analogy '— remote but real of Trinitarian truth.' See his work *Vie chrétienne et problèmes de la sexualitè* (Paris 1952), pp. 30, 32, etc. It may be mentioned that the Vatican, after approving the circulation of this work, forbade Roman Catholics to read it only a few months later (March 1953).

[15]According to Prof. K. Papapetrou, 'The conception that ethics judges according to a person's superficial behavior while psychology — especially depth psychology — goes to the depth of the human being, clearly derives from an inadmissable distinction between psychology and ethics. Ethics as the understanding of the human 'psyche' is psychology, just as psychology as the understanding of man is ethics.' (*Eccentrici as a Problem of Ontological Ethics* [Athens 1973], p. 28f).

[16]*Man for Himself* (London 1949), p. 7ff.

PART ONE
CHAPTER ONE

[1]As we know, every individual is 'unrepeatable' even biochemicaly. According to Eino Kaila, 'In accordance with the findings of contemporary physiological chemistry, every individual is unique in his chemical constitution' (D. Katz, ed., *Handbuch der Psychologie* [Basel 1951], p. 201). Also, according to H. Roth, it has been demonstrated by laboratory methods that 'no one is completely like anyone else' and that chemically and biologically every person constitutes a particular individuality,' H. Hetzer, ed., *Pädagogische Psychologie* [Gottingen 1959], p. 72).

[2]C. G. Jung, *Psychological types,* Collected works vol. 6, p. 448f.

[3]Adler takes an absolute position in the dispute between the conflicting views concerning the relative significance of heredity and environment in the educational process. 'So far as psychical phenomena and character traits are concerned, heredity plays a relatively unimportant role. There are no points of contact with reality which might support a theory of inherited character traits.' *Menschenkenntnis,* p. 130. *Understanding Human Nature,* transl. W. B. Wolfe, (London 1928), p. 163 (adapted).

[4]This idea was put forward and emphasized by depth psychology. Freud and Adler especially gave emphasis to the traumatic experiences of childhood, which, according to their view, are the causes of neurotic states in adults.

[5]It is characteristic that Fritz Riemann undertakes to define the result of the (traumatic) experiences of the first three months (!) of the life of a preacher in the content of his sermon. According to his view, emotional privations or attachments (due to psychical traumas) in the first stage of infancy determine the character of the indivual and, later, the way in which he thinks, as well as his emotional reactions. 'Die Persönlichkeit des Predigers aus tiefenpsychologischer Sicht,' in Richard Riess, ed., *Perspekstiven der Pastoralpsychologie* (Göttingen 1974), p. 153f.

[6]C. G. Jung, *The Structure and the Dynamics of the Psyche,* Collected works vol. 8, p. 18.

[7]C. G. Jung, *The Archetypes and the Collective Unconscious,* Collected works vol. 9, 1. p. 212f. See also Hans Schär, *Religion und Seele in der Psychologie C. G. Jungs* (Zurich 1946), p. 28.

[8]"According to the Apostle Paul, sin is a demonic power which entered into the world through Adam's transgression (Rom. 5, 12f) and established its kingdom within it, or more accurates, its tyranny, to which man fell victim as a slave and a subject. Man does not simply commit sin, but is, so to speak, "acted upon," led by it, because as a "captive" he serves it subject to the cruel law of its kingdom, which is death.' J. Karavidopoulos, *Sin according to the Apostle Paul* (Thessalonike 1968), p. 54f.

[9]The American historian Lancelot Whyte in his book *The Unconscious before Freud* (New York 1960) demonstrates that Freud was not the first to 'discover' the unconscious. Many thinkers and philosophers before him had shown a special interest in this dark region of the psyche. Among them he lists Kant, Hume, Descartes, Pascal, Marx, Nietzsche, Schopenhauer, Spinoza, Rousseau, Charcot, Dostoevsky, Hartmann, Bergson and others.

[10]See Freud's book *The Psychotherapy of Everyday Life,* tr. J. Strachey, Complete works vol. 6 (London 1960).

[11]According to Igor Caruso, 'Certainly Jung's psychology does not purport to be a theology. But it may admit of a sober conclusion which points to the possibility of restoring the psyche in its solitude into a frame of value references.' *Existential Psychology. From Analysis to Synthesis* (London 1964), p. xvii.

[12]*Understanding Human Nature,* p. 19 (adapted).

[13]Ibid. p. 20.

[14]Ibid. p. 75.

[15]Ibid. p. 165.

[16]*Our Inner Conflicts* (London 1946), p. 37.

[17]Ibid. p. 37.

[18]Ibid. p. 38.

[19]Ibid. p. 40.

[20]Ibid. p. 38.

[21]Ibid. p. 96.

[22]Ibid. p. 46.

[23]Ibid. p. 96.

[24]Ibid. p. 97.

[25]Ibid.

[26]Ibid. p. 98f.

[27]According to the psychiatrist who translated Horney's book into Greek, 'K. Horney, on the contrary, gives an important place to moral values, because she believes that we cannot make a science of personality without a science of human values.' Ibid. p. 16.

[28]K. Horney, *Neurosis and human growth. The Struggle toward Self Realization* (London 1951), p. 14.

[29]*Our Inner Conflicts,* p. 23f.

[30]*Bios Psyche Person* (Freiburg-München 1957).

[31]*Existential Psychology* (London 1964).

[32]Ibid. p. 64.

[33]Ibid. p. 60.

[34]Ibid. p. 66.

[35]Ibid. p. 61.

[36]With the passage of time the application of the basic principles of depth psychology to the field of psychotherapy is demonstrating more and more clearly the indissoluble relation between the psychic factor and the moral awareness of the individual. According to Erich Fromm, 'Neurosis itself is, in the last analysis, a symptom of moral failure . . . In many instances a neurotic symptom is the specific expression of moral conflict, and the success of the therapeutic effort depends on the understanding and solution of the moral problem of the individual.' *Man for Himself. An Inquiry into the Psychology of Ethics* (London 1949), p. viii.

CHAPTER TWO

[1]According to Wolfgang Kretschmer, 'The shame which a man feels because he is "individual" comes from the guilt which everyone experiences who is separated from God,' *Psychologische Weisheit der Bibel* (Munich 1955), p. 175. On the other hand, according to Erich Fromm the transgression of God's will (the ancestral sin) is 'the beginning of human freedom.' 'Acting against God's command means freeing himself from coercion, emerging from the unconscious existence of prehuman life to the level of man. Acting against the commands the authority, committing a sin, in its positive human aspect the first act of freedom, that is, the first *human* act,' (*Fear of Freedom* [London 1942], p. 27). This difference of views is understandably due to the contrast between the world views of the two thinkers. The first represents the Christian view and understands the concept 'individual' as lacking the free expression of the human person. The second, faithful to the basic position of psychoanalysis, sees the ancestral sin as an act which establishes human freedom.

[2]An example of this *a posteriori* attempt to understand the state of adamic man before the Fall 'there is peace and repose; but at the same time there is something different, which is not dissension and strife, for there is nothing to strive with. What is it then? Nothing. But what effects does it produce? It begets dread. This is the profound secret of innocence, that at the same time it is dread . . . The dread which is posited in innocence is, in the first place, not guilt; in the second place, it is not a heavy burden, not a suffering which cannot be brought into harmony with the felicity of innocence . . . When we consider the dialectical determinants in dread, it appears that they have precisely the characteristic ambiguity of psychology. Dread is a *sympathetic antipathy and an antipathetic sympathy.*' S. Kierkegard, *The Concept of Dread* (London 1944), p. 38. Kierkegaard 'struggles' to present the innocence before the Fall as a state with 'dialectical determinants,' that is, in opposition. Consequently in his thoughts the concept of a conflict is latent, but with a 'positive' character.

[3]Because the concept of this choice has strongly opposing elements in its structure (either the 'one' or the 'other'), it is regarded as a fundamental conflict and is characterized in the tradition and life of the Church as 'temptation.' Temptation as a psychic conflict can have one or the other outcome.

[4]The word 'prohibition' is the great trouble-maker in Freudian psychoanalysis. 'Prohibition' as a limitation of man's expression and self-determination is seen, as a rule, as 'the blockage of freedom' which 'turns man's instincts backwards against man himself,' (Erich Fromm, *Man for Himself. An Inquiry into the Psychology of Ethics* [London 1949], p. 151). But under the conditions of life of the adamic couple the *prohibition* can only be understood as a way of expressing and vouchsafing his freedom.

[5]Fromm clearly underlines the antithetic functioning of the egoistic drives: 'The selfish person does not love himself too much but too little, in fact he hates himself,' *Man for Himself*, p. 131.

[6]See P. Daco, *Les triomphes de la psychoanalyse*. Greek translation. (Athens 1970), p. 467.

[7]The anthropomorphic character of the presence of God in the adamic drama helps Freudian psychoanalysis to characterize the conscience as *interiorized* authority. But that cannot cast a suspicion of Freudian tendencies upon the acceptance of Adam's conscience as functioning 'in the person of God.'

[8]As to the origin of fear, it may be recalled that Kierkegaard traces it to the state of innocence which begets dread, before the Fall. In this state fear can be identified with the dread which 'is the reality of freedom as possibility' (*The concept of dread*, p. 38). Erich Fromm, in his work *Fear of Freedom,* explains better the possibility of a correlation between fear of freedom and the dread which, according to Kierkegaard, stems from the adamic innocence before the Fall.

[9]J. K. Kornarakis, *Neurosis as the 'Adamic Complex'* (Thessalonike 1966).

[10]The primary conflict, from the moment of its formation, is relived every time the individual is faced with an axiological choice. Adam's preference to be expelled from Paradise rather than accept his guilt and confess it with contrition and repentance is a repetition of his unfortunate axiological choice. This means, according to Caruso, that the neurotic person makes a relative value into an absolute and inverted one, and especially that the 'bad' conscience is made into an absolute (normative) value in life. See Kornarakis *(Neurosis as the 'Adam Complex,'* p. 66f).

[11]Helmut Harsch too speaks of 'existential guilt,' which must be distinguished from the *concrete sin* (Tätsünde) which separates men from God. 'Existential guilt' (*Existenzschuld*), he says, is the main target of anthropological psychotherapy. (See his study 'Die Bedeutung des Tiefenpsychologisches Schuldverständnisses für die Theologie' in *Perspektiven der Pastoralpsychologie,* ed. R. Riess [Göttingen 1974], p. 46.)

[12]From the psychoanalytic point of view a symptom is the *compensation* for a psychic function which, through being repressed, has not developed fully. The symptom, then, is an indicator of the form and nature of the conflict, which in any case is connected with a strong repression. For this reason the study of the form and nature of the symptom leads us to an understanding of the conflict. See P. Daco, *Les triomphes de la psychoanalyse* (in Greek transl.) pp. 56 and 550f.

[13]*Man for Himself,* p. 151.

[14]Clinical experience convinces K. Horney that 'usually the mere recognition of a neurotic trend does not engender any radical change. In the first place, the willingness to change which is elicited by the discovery of such a trend is equivocal

and hence lacks forcefulness and, in the second place, a willingness to change, even if it amounts to an unambiguous wish, is not yet an ability to change. This ability develops only later,' *Self-analysis* (London 1942), p. 90.

[15]The reader can find two examples of cases which demonstrate the 'blindness' of the analyst to the guilt problem of his neurotic patient in our book *Neurosis as the Adam Complex*, p. 56f.

[16]P. Daco, *Les prodigieuses victoires de la psychologie moderne* (Verviers, Belgium 1960), p. 140f.

[17]Ibid. p. 141.

[18]Ibid. p. 188.

[19]For the 'scapegoat complex' see my book *Biblical Psychographs* (Thessalonike 1975), p. 120 (in Greek).

PART TWO
CHAPTER ONE

[1]The Roman Catholic pastoral psychologist Albert Niedermeyer offers a 'catholic psychotherapy,' using the word 'catholic' in the sense of 'universal.' According to this view, the pastoral approach to man makes use of *biological* and *social* data (instincts, deposits, environment) just as much as moral and metaphysical perspectives. See *Handbuch der speziellen Pastoralmedizin Psychopathologie und Psychotherapie*, 5th ed. (Vienna 1952), pp. 240 and 263.

[2]The Pharisee absolutizes the outward religious forms because of his inner conflict. Consequently his religious feeling is absolutized through his one-sided attachment to these forms. According to Caruso, 'In absolutizing his own emotions and perceptions, the neurotic is in the first instance prone to a specific *greed for experience*. . . Only by constant experience can the neurotic prove to himself that he is alive at all . . . Thus the neurotic is led, to an evil "transcendence": he is compelled to look for corroboration of the value of life outside, in objects, and placed in a position of intolerable dependence on the things of this world,' *Existential psychology* (London 1964), p. 44.

[3]According to A. Maillot, 'A Pharisee is not one who feels righteous but one who justifies himself at the expense of others,' *Les parables de Jésus aujourd'hui*, p. 200.

[4]According to K. Horney, 'In all its essentials the idealized image is an unconscious phenomenon. Although his self-inflation may be most obvious even to an untrained observer, the neurotic is not aware that he is idealizing himself. Nor does he know what a bizarre conglomeration of characters is assembled here. He may have a vague sense that he is making high demands upon himself, but mistaking such perfectionist demands for genuine ideals, he in no way questions their validity and is indeed rather proud of them.' *Our Inner Conflicts*, p. 97.

[5]The personal unconscious, as Jung understands it, is filled with repressions which in some way form 'receptive representations,' or, more accurately, 'receptive experiences.' These repressions gather in 'associations of experiences' that are activated according to the challenges which the personal unconscious receives through the experiences of our personality.

[7]According to J. Chrysostom the Pharisee's behavior is manifested as a 'mad passion' against human nature in general. 'Oh what a mad passion . . . All human

nature was not enough to satisfy his madness, and he furiously attacked the tax collector who was standing near.' PG 48.745.

[8]As we know, the occasion for the Lord's narration of the parable was the humiliating behavior which 'some who trusted in themselves that they were righteous' (Lk 18.9) showed towards their neighbours.

[9]*Biblical Psychographs*, p. 21.

[10]*Our Inner Conflicts*, p. 73.

[11]Ibid. p. 74.

[12]Ibid. p. 75.

[13]Ibid. p. 77.

[14]Ibid. p. 80.

[15]Ibid. p. 75.

[16]Ibid. p. 94.

[17]This guilt is not 'stored' in the personal unconscious in complete functional isolation, so it reacts with its own 'will' to stimuli coming from outside. Because of the unconscious character of *repression,* this guilt forms a link in a chain of 'guilty associations.' Hence its bearer is threatened with becoming conscious of it whenever his experiences relate to 'homogeneous' guilty associations.

[18]*Our Inner Conflicts*, p. 75.

[19]Ibid. p. 77.

[20]Ibid. p. 81f.

[21]Ibid. p. 76.

[22]Ibid. p. 80.

[23]Ibid. p. 91.

[24]'Transference' is an unconscious psychic phenomenon (or 'psychic mechanism') which is manifested mainly during the development of the psychoanalytic dialogue. The analyst is always ready to accept a 'transference' on the part of his client and in fact knows that at certain crucial points in this development he himself must incite such a reaction in him.

[25]Fromm rightly observes: 'This irrational fear of death (not the normal fear of having to die which every human being experiences in the contemplation of death) results from the failure to have lived, it is the expression of our guilty conscience for having wasted our life and missed the chance of productive use of our capacities. To die is poignantly bitter, but the idea of having to die without having lived is unbearable,' *Man for Himself,* p. 162.

[26]P. Bratsiotis's article in *Megali Elliniki Enkyklopaideia,* 2nd ed., vol. 13, p. 103.

[27]W. Bauer, *Das Leben Jesu im Zeitalter der neutestamentlichen Apokrypha* (Tübungen 1909), p. 174.

[28]J. Kornarakis, *Judas as an Archetype of Collective Guilt* (Thessalonike 1977), p. 70f.

[29]Ibid. p. 137f.

[30]C. G. Jung, *Symbols of transformation,* Collected works vol. 5, p. 304, J. Kornarakis, *Judas . . .* p. 138f.

[31]It is indicative that the debtor servant would have had to be sold with his

family in order to 'repay' his debt to his master. This fact shows that this debt had an existential meaning and not the meaning of any ordinary financial or material business.

[32]*Our Inner Conflicts,* p. 119.

[33]*Current Perspectives on Social Psychology,* ed. E.P. Hollander and R.G. Hunt, 4th ed, Oxford 1976, contains special sections on the differentiation of roles and the role conflicts arising from this differentiation (p. 283f and 286).

[34]See Leon Mann *Social Psychology* (London 1969), especially p. 33f. Likewise H.C. Lingren, *An Introduction to Social Psychology* (London 1969).

[35]See H. Bergson, *The Two Sources of Morality and Religion* (London 1935), p. 1f.

[36]Karen Horney speaks at length about impoverishment of personality, of which bodily fatigue is a characteristic feature. *Our Inner Conflicts,* p. 155 and 159f.

[37]As we know, the biblical text presents the twin brothers Esau and Jacob as rivals already from their birth. 'The first came out red. He was like a hairy garment all over; so they called his name Essau. Afterwards his brother came out, and his hand took hold of Esau's heel; so his name was called Jacob' (Gen 25.25f).

[38]Prof. Hans Hoff accepts that the psychic trauma due to the absence of emotional contanct with the mother can be 'the beginning of later neurotic or psychopathic behavior.' *Lehrbuch der Psychiatrie,* vol 2 (Basel—Stuttgart 1956), p. 556.

[39]See A. Vetter. *Wirklichkeit des Menschlichens* (Munich 1960), p. 31.

[40]It is known that in his fundamental work *Understanding Human Nature* Adler brought out with characteristic psychological clarity the particular phases of the rivalry between siblings, which comes about mainly through the order in which they are born.

[41]Philipp Lersch reminds us that in certain cases the psychological dialogue with the role is a painful inner trial, *Der Mensch als soziales Wesen,* (Munich 1964), p. 161ff. The bearer of the role is under psychological pressure to play his role. Insofar as he encounters difficulties, he is in conflict with these difficulties, i.e. with himself.

[42]*Biblical Psychographs,* p. 112f.

[43]The work of Christa Meves *Die Bibel antwortet uns in Bildern,* 3rd ed. (Ffreiburg 1973), p. 42ff presents a characteristic form of escape from responsibilities through the return of the individual to the chaos of the unconscious, which is lived as a 'reactive depression.'

[44]As we have said, the Viennese psychiatrist Igor Caruso emphasizes that a severe inner conflict is inevitably expressed as 'absolutizing the relative and relativizing the absolute' in the individual's relations with the values of life. The absolutization of a 'mess of pottage' is always, beyond doubt, a symptom of a severe inner conflict.

CHAPTER TWO

[1]The total view of human existence is a fundamental principle for pastoral psychology. According to H. Schmidt, 'It would be a fatal error, if one attempted to build one's religious life exclusively on the purely spiritual basis of

intellectual understanding and of the readiness of the will, thus excluding the lower psychic powers . . . Sound Christian ascetics must take into account the law of the totality of organic doctrine, according to which all powers and capabilities of the soul, the higher and lower ones alike, must be the servants of God,' see W. Demal, *Pastoral Psychology in Practice*, trans. J. W. Conway (Cork and New York 1955), p. 21.

[2]*Psychiatric Morale Experimentale Individuelle et social* (Paris 1950), p. 208.

[3]Lev. 16,8-10; 21-22, 26.

[4]Most Christians know the Lord's parable of the Prodigal Son recorded by Luke the Evangelist (15,11-32). For this theme see J. Karavidopoulos, *The Parables of Jesus* (Thessalonike 1970), p. 128f, and J. Kornarakis, *Biblical Psychographs*, p. 32, note 2.

[5]According to Robert W. White, the human being has a strong innate tendency towards self-sufficiency and self-determination; by dint of those he resists influence from the outside on the one hand and subjects heteronomous powers of the natural and social environment to his sphere of influence on the other hand. But since the heteronomous powers (in their totality) are indomitable, the individual finally capitulates to the pressure of these powers. *Current Perspectives in Social Psychology*, ed. E. Hollander and R. Hunt (Toronto 1971), p. 32.

[6]According to Maillot, 'far . . . far is always the place of freedom. Far and tomorrow . . . are the great words of human nostalgia. Success is always located in the magic of the future. But this nostalgia is ambiguous.' *Les parables de Jesus aujourd'hui* (Geneva 1973), p. 142.

[7]According to Michel Adam, 'sin is surrender to ease' (*à la facilité*). (*Le sentiment du peche. Etude de psychologie* [Paris 1967], p. 113). But such a surrender obviously involves a waste of psychic and spiritual powers. See also Karen Horney, *Our Inner Conflicts*, p. 155.

[8]*Fear of Freedom*, p. 155.

[9]Ibid. p. 106.

[10]As we know, the fundamental purpose of psychotherapeutic methodology is to make the neurotic person *conscious* of the repressions and psychic traumas in general in his past life. The prodigal son seems to have reached this awareness by self-examination. It is characteristic that Maillot translates the phrase 'when he came to himself' as 'when he came to the depth of himself,' (*Les parables*, p. 148.).

[11]The element of sacrifice in repentance has no connection with the neurotic's self punishment (*Selbstbestrafung*), by which he attempts to make expiation. Freud correlates the problem of guilt with self punishment. But we must understand the self sacrifice of the prodigal son as a free act arising from the redemptive effect of a positive solution of the basic psychic problem. In the case of the neurotic, self sacrifice (as punishment) aims at reducing the intensity of the feeling of guilt. But this is equivalent to a 'false solution' of this guilt problem, see H. Harsch, *Das Schuldproblem in Theologie und tiefen Psychologie*, p. 68f.

[12]The simplicity of the publican's behavior expresses his innocence at the same time. According to M. Adam, 'Innocence is absence of problems,' p. 24f.

[13]Hans Hoff, *Lehrbuch der Psychiatrie* (Basel 1956), vol. 2, pp. 617 and 629.

[14]*Angst und Schuld in theologischen und psychotherapeutischer Sicht*, ed. W. Bitter (Struggart 1967), p. 88, article by Vera Scheffen, "Organic neurosis as a

consequence of anxiety and guilt''.

[15]Albert Niedermeyer, citing Moerchen's view, maintains that personal guilt contributes to the making of the hysterical character (op. cit, vol. 5, p. 86f).

[16]Victor of Antioch puts the following words on the lips of the Lord: 'I know what they do not see. The soul is ill before the body. Accordingly I shall heal the cause of the illness.' J. A. Cramer, ed., *Catenae Graecorum patrum*, vol. 1, p. 285.

[17]See J. Kornarakis, *Neurosis as Adam Complex*, p. 9.

[18]Only the Evangelist Matthew quotes 'Take heart, my son.' See J. Kornarakis, *Biblical Psychographs*, p. 38.

[19]In his small book *Katholische Beichte und Psychotherapie* (Innsbruck-Vienna 1947), p. 12, O. J. Miller S. J. compares two examples of the healing of paralysis after personal guilt was made conscious. The examples are taken from E. Grünewald's book *Flucht in die Krankheit?*, (Innsbruck 1947). We give the first one in brief. 'A young woman of 25 came for therapy to the neurological section because she was suffering from paralysis of the lower limbs. But the neurological examination did not reveal anything special. After the third meeting with the psychotherapist she was persuaded to 'talk' and she told the following story of her life. After she became engaged, her fiance happened to be away in a distant city for quite a time. During this absence the young woman formed a new and hence 'illicit' relationship. It was a relationship with a married man, with whom she finally began to have sexual intercourse. During this illicit relationship she received a letter from her fiance, who informed her that he would shortly come back for their wedding. With this letter she felt an intolerable guilt and she tried to break off her illicit relationship. But her married friend reacted in such a way as to persuade her to continue their intimacy. As the time approached for her fiance's return, she became stricken with fear at the thought that this man was coming and would find out about her unfaithfulness and her moral inferiority.

While she was in the grip of this psychic state, she was involved in a traffic accident from which she barely escaped with her life. She was taken to hospital, where she was found to be unable to walk. All the medical examinations failed to discover an organic cause for the weakness of her lower limbs. The conclusion, then, was obvious. It was a psychogenic paralysis which had the meaning of a 'flight into sickness,' i.e. 'flight from responsibility.' The paralysis was used unconsciously as a 'means to an end.'

The psychotherapist analyzed the connection in this woman between her bodily paralysis and her psychological (moral) problem and she understood that her solution to this problem had been a superficial one and that by her 'illness' she was lying to three people: her fiance, her friend, and herself.

INDEX